THE UPPER ROOM

WHERE THE WORLD MEETS TO PRAY

Daniele Och

UK editor

INVITATIONAL

INTERDENOMINATIONAL

INTERNATIONAL

34 LANGUAGES

Multiple formats are available in some languages

 **BRF** Ministries

15 The Chambers, Vineyard
Abingdon OX14 3FE
brf.org.uk

Bible Reading Fellowship (BRF) is a charity (233280)
and company limited by guarantee (301324),
registered in England and Wales

ISBN 978 1 80039 261 8
All rights reserved

Originally published in the USA by The Upper Room® **upperroom.org**
US edition © 2023 The Upper Room, Nashville, TN (USA). All rights reserved.
This edition © Bible Reading Fellowship 2023
Cover photo by Julia Volk/pexels.com

Acknowledgements

Scripture quotations marked with the following abbreviations are taken from the
version shown. Where no abbreviation is given, the quotation is taken from the same
version as the headline reference.

NIV: The Holy Bible, New International Version (Anglicised edition) copyright © 1979,
1984, 2011 by Biblica. Used by permission of Hodder & Stoughton Publishers, an
Hachette UK company. All rights reserved. 'NIV' is a registered trademark of Biblica.
UK trademark number 1448790.

NRSV: The New Revised Standard Version Updated Edition. Copyright © 2021
National Council of Churches of Christ in the United States of America. Used by
permission. All rights reserved worldwide.

CEB: copyright © 2011 by Common English Bible.

KJV: the Authorised Version of the Bible (The King James Bible), the rights in which
are vested in the Crown, are reproduced by permission of the Crown's Patentee,
Cambridge University Press.

A catalogue record for this book is available from the British Library

Printed by Gutenberg Press, Tarxien, Malta

How to use *The Upper Room*

The Upper Room is ideal in helping us spend a quiet time with God each day. Each daily entry is based on a passage of scripture and is followed by a meditation and prayer. Each person who contributes a meditation seeks to relate their experience of God in a way that will help those who use *The Upper Room* every day.

Here are some guidelines to help you make best use of *The Upper Room*:

1 Read the passage of scripture. It is a good idea to read it more than once, in order to have a fuller understanding of what it is about and what you can learn from it.
2 Read the meditation. How does it relate to your own experience? Can you identify with what the writer has outlined from their own experience or understanding?
3 Pray the written prayer. Think about how you can use it to relate to people you know or situations that need your prayers today.
4 Think about the contributor who has written the meditation. Some users of *The Upper Room* include this person in their prayers for the day.
5 Meditate on the 'Thought for the day' and the 'Prayer focus', perhaps using them again as the focus for prayer or direction for action.

Why is it important to have a daily quiet time? Many people will agree that it is the best way of keeping in touch every day with the God who sustains us and who sends us out to do his will and show his love to the people we encounter each day. Meeting with God in this way reassures us of his presence with us, helps us to discern his will for us and makes us part of his worldwide family of Christian people through our prayers.

I hope that you will be encouraged as you use *The Upper Room* regularly as part of your daily devotions, and that God will richly bless you as you read his word and seek to learn more about him.

Helping to pay it forward

As part of our Living Faith ministry, we're raising funds to give away copies of Bible reading notes and other resources to those who aren't able to access them any other way, working with food banks and chaplaincy services, in prisons, hospitals and care homes. If you've enjoyed and benefited from our resources, would you consider paying it forward to enable others to do so too?

Make a gift at **brf.org.uk/donate**

thank
you

for all your support

Bridge builder

There is one lawgiver and judge who is able to save and to destroy. So who, then, are you to judge your neighbour?
James 4:12 (NRSV)

Both Jewish and Christian scholars assert that James functioned as a righteous teacher and bridge builder between Jewish followers of his brother Jesus and those who adhered to the tenets of emerging rabbinic Judaism. James pointed to the heart of scripture when he wrote, 'If you really fulfil the royal law according to the scripture, "You shall love your neighbour as yourself," you do well' (James 2:8). His words continue to offer guidance for bridge building today.

In his writings, James taught that Jesus' followers are distinguished by their non-judgemental posture towards others. He instructed, 'Let everyone be quick to listen, slow to speak, slow to anger, for human anger does not produce God's righteousness' (James 1:19–20). James also taught that when we draw near to God, God will draw near to us (James 4:8) and empower us to show mercy instead of judgement and to listen with compassion before offering advice.

In a world that constantly tempts us to embrace division, anger and fear, what would our new year look like if we chose to live according to the humble example of James, our ancient brother in Christ? What arguments might end? What truths might we find? What aspects of our most authentic selves might joyfully emerge?

Kimberly Orr
World editor and publisher

Bulgarian edition

Polish edition

Writers featured in this issue of *The Upper Room*:

• Hadassah Treu (Bulgaria) • Madeline Kalu (Germany)
• Jolanta Burzynska (Poland)

Gifts to the international editions
of *The Upper Room* help the world
meet to pray. **upperroom.org/gift**

The editor writes...

Let us therefore approach the throne of grace with boldness, so that we may receive mercy and find grace to help in time of need.
Hebrews 4:16 (NRSV)

If I were to compile a list of favourite verses and passages from the Bible, Hebrews 4:16 would be among them, largely thanks to a sermon that I once heard on it many years ago. One of the many riches of this verse is the injunction to 'approach the throne... with boldness'. As I first learned in that sermon, the word translated 'boldness' is *parrhesia*, which can be literally translated as 'speak everything'. To the ancient Greeks, *parrhesia* referred to the right of a citizen to freely speak at the public assembly without fear of recrimination.

To exercise your right to say what you like among your fellow citizens is one thing; to do so before a throne – that is, before a ruler who has the power of life and death over you – is quite another. If there were ever a time when you would want to choose your words carefully, that would be it.

And yet when it comes to not just *a* throne, but *the* throne – the throne of God – the writer to the Hebrews urges us to feel free to 'speak everything', to express whatever is on our hearts and minds. When before God's throne, we do not have to choose our words carefully for fear of recrimination if we cause offence. This is because God's throne is 'the throne of grace', which we can approach because, as the preceding verses explain, 'we have a great high priest... Jesus, the Son of God' (v. 14).

In each issue of *The Upper Room*, the meditations cover a wide range of experience and emotion. While it is true that most, if not all, of the following meditations express praise, thanks and trust in the Lord, many of them do so in the midst of, or after a time of, anxiety, pain, anguish or perplexity.

So as you use this issue as part of your devotional time, hear God's invitation to you to draw near to the throne of grace and 'speak everything' – joy or sadness, delight or anger, thanksgiving or confusion, or even just some random trivia. And in doing so, may you receive mercy and find grace.

Daniele Och, UK editor

Speak a new beginning

Read John 1:1–9

God said, 'Let there be light,' and there was light.
Genesis 1:3 (NRSV)

I felt extremely grateful at the New Year's Eve service in 2021. It indeed felt like a new beginning, a new hope against the odds of the past year. Yet after the service, I was in tears as I thought of all the things I didn't have. I wanted so much for the new year, but I didn't know how or where to start. I felt hopeless.

That night, I decided to pray again. I didn't ask for anything. Instead, inspired by 1 Thessalonians 5:18, I gave thanks for all that I had, and I felt blessed by everything on my list. After this prayer of gratitude, I had Genesis 1:3 in my heart and a new understanding of the verse. In Genesis 1:1–2 it was the beginning, and it looked hopeless. In that bleak situation, God spoke light. With that light came hope, and God kept speaking, forming sky, seas and land. What God wanted for the future, day after day, God spoke into being. Until it was all good, God spoke.

As believers, when faced with a hopeless situation, the first thing we can do is invite the light into that situation. We can speak: 'Thank you, Jesus.' He is the light of the world (see John 8:12). With Christ's light comes hope. My resolution this year is to speak light through all my days.

Prayer: *Dear God, help us to be grateful in all situations. Show us how to speak light and goodness into our lives and the lives of those around us. Amen.*

Thought for the day: With the light of Christ comes great hope.

P. E. Uloh (Edo, Nigeria)

Standing tall

Read Romans 5:1–5

Consider it pure joy, my brothers and sisters, whenever you face trials of many kinds, because you know that the testing of your faith produces perseverance.

James 1:2–3 (NIV)

When we moved to our current home, we learned that the redbud tree is very common here. They are often oddly shaped with gnarled trunks. Many have broken branches from storm damage. But in the spring, they are the first trees to bud; when their flowers open, they bring vibrant colour to the dull, winter landscape.

One autumn, my husband transplanted a redbud sapling into our yard. Within a few months, a storm had broken its tallest branch. However, the young tree made it through the winter, and its remaining branch bloomed in the spring. It continues to grow tall to this day. God made the redbud tree to withstand all sorts of adversity, and it continues to be resilient.

I want to be like those beautiful trees. When I am faced with hardship, I want to trust in God my creator. God has much good planned for us and can turn our struggles into blessings if we persevere. When hard times attack me, I want to be strong enough to say, 'You are helpless against me because God made me and I can overcome anything through God's power.' With this faith I can stand tall like the steadfast redbud trees.

Prayer: *Father God, thank you for models of resilience and strength in nature. Empower us to persevere through our struggles. Amen.*

Thought for the day: I can rely on God for resilience and strength.

Janet Kratochvil (Indiana, USA)

Sense of purpose

Read 1 Thessalonians 5:12–23

Rejoice always, pray without ceasing, give thanks in all circumstances, for this is the will of God in Christ Jesus for you.
1 Thessalonians 5:16–18 (NRSV)

I didn't intend to retire, but I lost my job at 64. Then we moved because my husband changed jobs. Shortly after our relocation, I was able to take two extended trips to be with a family member in crisis and later to welcome my new grandson. These would not have been possible had I started a new job. But I missed the sense of purpose and the structure that my profession had provided, and I wasn't sure how to fill my days. I realised that I could keep mourning what I had lost or choose to actively nurture a new sense of purpose for my life.

We choose each day how to live out our discipleship. I do not believe there are days when nothing important happens. Paul reminds us in 1 Thessalonians of God's will for our lives: we are to rejoice always, pray constantly and give thanks in all circumstances. But such simple directives are impossible to follow when we focus on what is wrong rather than on what is right.

I now choose to begin and end my day in prayerful reflection, paying attention to the goodness of God that surrounds me. I review the day with gratitude – even the parts that were difficult – and deliberately name the joys. When I choose to rejoice, pray and give thanks, I can see beyond my circumstances, and my heart is oriented towards God's purpose.

Prayer: *O God, we pray that our words and actions will reflect gratitude for your presence and provision on this day. In Jesus' name. Amen.*

Thought for the day: My faith in God gives my life purpose.

Linda Coggin (British Columbia, Canada)

The power of love

Read Titus 3:4–8

How priceless is your unfailing love, O God! People take refuge in the shadow of your wings.
Psalm 36:7 (NIV)

When our family relocated to the desert southwest, about the only relief from the relentless heat of the summer months was a trip to the public swimming pool. My parents enrolled my brothers and me in swimming lessons. I can still recall the fear during some of those first lessons, especially when we were taken into the deep end of the pool. But our instructors were kind, and we trusted them to keep us safe.

Many years later, my wife and I had three small children of our own, and we needed to teach them to swim so that they could be safe in and near the water. My wife, being a certified water safety instructor, taught them. I recall some thrashing, splashing and even some crying, but our children knew their teacher was always there to support them and keep them safe from danger, and she would not let them go. Eventually my children swam very well, competed on swim teams and were rewarded with ribbons and trophies.

Now, in my later years, I sometimes reflect on how those swim lessons are similar to my relationship with God who is my teacher and is worthy of all my trust. Yet there are times when I thrash about and feel consumed by fear. But then I remember that God is love and will not let me go.

Prayer: *Dear God, thank you for your everlasting love that surpasses our understanding. Help us to remain devoted to you. In Jesus' name we pray. Amen.*

Thought for the day: God will never let me go.

Doug Wingert (Arizona, USA)

Intent on giving

Read Philippians 2:1–11

Do nothing from selfish ambition or empty conceit, but in humility regard others as better than yourselves. Let each of you look not to your own interests but to the interests of others.
Philippians 2:3–4 (NRSV)

After a snowstorm and dramatic drop in temperature, a thick layer of ice and snow covered the ground. Although it was blisteringly cold, my husband, Solomon, went out to clear the sidewalk in front of our house. It was hard work, but he slowly began to carve a path.

Solomon had leaned back on his shovel to take a brief break when a man passed by. He was dressed inadequately for the weather and looked gaunt, but he offered to help Solomon shovel the snow and did so with gusto. As the man shovelled snow, he and my husband struck up a conversation. Upon hearing that the man was homeless, Solomon's heart was grieved. He knew that during the harsh winter, many people were in dire need of shelter and provision, yet this stranger had approached Solomon with a heart intent on giving. Working together, they cleared the sidewalk. In return for his kindness, Solomon gave the man a gift before bidding him farewell.

Afterward, Solomon ruminated on the lesson God had shown him – that help can come in unexpected ways and we should be open to receiving it. We each have God-given gifts that we can use to lift each other up and provide hope.

Prayer: *Merciful Father, help us to receive the gifts and assistance of others. Show us how to use our gifts to provide hope and help to those around us. In Jesus' name. Amen.*

Thought for the day: Each of us has gifts that can benefit others.

Madeline Kalu (North Rhine-Westphalia, Germany)

One day at a time

Read Psalm 55:1–8, 16–19
Cast your burden on the Lord, and he will sustain you; he will never permit the righteous to be moved.
Psalm 55:22 (NRSV)

When I lost my job, my family lost our only source of income. Anxiety and worry overcame me, and I felt the weight of the world on me. The only thought in my mind was, *What now?*

I had always read my Bible daily, and as I read the many passages about worry, I remembered what I had always known but had temporarily forgotten: when we trust God, life will not break us. All troubles are temporary, but God's loving care lasts forever. Knowing this and living according to this truth made all the difference. Instead of worry driving us apart, our family grew closer, and we learned how to adapt and overcome. A better and calmer outlook on life made it easier to endure hardship, make new friends and build a new life from the wreckage of the old.

Eventually I did get another job and got back on my feet. And while I would not like to go through the experience again, I learned a valuable lesson that I might not have in any other way. Worrying about what might be down the road can only hurt us, but trust in the Lord always heals us – one step and one day at a time.

Prayer: *Dear Lord, thank you for assuring us that we never have to be consumed by worry because you will meet our deepest needs. Amen.*

Thought for the day: Life may bend me, but God's sustaining love will uphold me.

Mark A. Carter (Oregon, USA)

God provides

Read 1 Kings 17:7–16

My God will meet your every need out of his riches in the glory that is found in Christ Jesus.
Philippians 4:19 (CEB)

When a great drought hit, the water pump in our house broke. My parents didn't have the money to buy a new one. We prayed constantly for rain, but the rain didn't come.

We cannot live without water. But thankfully some neighbours who had sophisticated water pumps with sufficient water supply offered to help. They allowed my family to take as much water as we needed. So every day my parents and I carried buckets to the neighbours' houses to fetch water until the dry season was over.

This experience was a reminder to me that God doesn't always answer prayers the way we want or expect. It didn't rain immediately after we prayed. But God answered our prayers according to our needs by bringing us kind-hearted neighbours to provide water for us to use every day.

Prayer: *God our provider, help us to trust that you will answer our prayers even if the answer is not what we expect. We give thanks for the help you offer us and pray as Jesus taught us: 'Our Father which art in heaven, Hallowed be thy name. Thy kingdom come, Thy will be done in earth, as it is in heaven. Give us this day our daily bread. And forgive us our debts, as we forgive our debtors. And lead us not into temptation, but deliver us from evil: For thine is the kingdom, and the power, and the glory, forever. Amen' (Matthew 6:9–13, KJV).*

Thought for the day: God provides for my needs.

Juita Kartini (Jakarta, Indonesia)

Blessings within burdens

Read John 11:32–44

We know that in all things God works for the good of those who love him.
Romans 8:28 (NIV)

At age 22, our son, John, who had Duchenne muscular dystrophy, had surgery to insert feeding tubes. Loss of muscles, including those that control swallowing, created a condition that contributed to frequent pneumonia. John had also lost weight.

Two months after the surgery, with Thanksgiving approaching, I felt despondent because John could no longer join in family meals with us. The scripture reading at church about Jesus' raising Lazarus from the dead took on new meaning, however. Instead of lamenting that John couldn't eat, I thanked God that he was alive. How wonderful that God gave people the knowledge and skill to put all nutrients needed to sustain human life in a can!

John could not enjoy family meals as he once had, but he could laugh, talk, play games, defend his views, give advice, tell jokes and watch his favourite football team. Although the ingenuity underlying tube-feeding that restored his life differed markedly from Christ's miraculous raising of Lazarus, it allowed John to be with us for eleven more years and live to see his younger sisters become adults.

Prayer: *Dear God, thank you for helping us see how you can use even heavy burdens to restore life. Help us live one day at a time, trusting you to provide for us. In Jesus' name. Amen.*

Thought for the day: Hidden blessings can be found in heavy burdens.

Margaret Foegen Karsten (Wisconsin, USA)

PRAYER FOCUS: THOSE WITH MUSCULAR DYSTROPHY

God is our guide

Read Psalm 16

You teach me the way of life. In your presence is total celebration.
Psalm 16:11 (CEB)

I remember one time when my children were young, we walked a maze. We followed the walled path. When we neared what we thought was the exit, there was another wall. We had to back up and look for another way out. It was a bit difficult to reach the end, but with perseverance we reached the goal.

Life is like a maze. Many times, we ask God why certain things happen to us. We try to grasp situations but are unable to understand them. We hurry here and there looking for the right path. Obstacles stop us in our tracks, and we don't understand why we must backtrack or even face those obstacles in the first place. It becomes crucial to allow God to guide us through the twisting and turning passageways of life so that we can find the path that will lead to the fullness of joy that only God can offer.

Prayer: *Almighty God, show us the path that leads to the fullness of joy in you. In Jesus' name we pray. Amen.*

Thought for the day: God will faithfully guide me.

Nelly R. Reina (Córdoba, Argentina)

Before we ask

Read Ephesians 3:14–21

Let us hold fast the profession of our faith without wavering; (for he is faithful that promised).
Hebrews 10:23 (KJV)

As I write, my beloved wife is undergoing her seventh surgery for breast cancer in just over three years. She has also endured 13 months of chemotherapy. After checking in at the hospital this morning, we prayed together.

Once she was taken back for anaesthesia and surgery, I prayed earnestly for her and for all the doctors, nurses and technicians involved in her surgery. I then read my daily devotional. When I completed that reading, it occurred to me that in my prayer life I have asked for many things. Although I do thank God for the gift of grace through Jesus Christ and for the many blessings of my life, I feel as though most of my prayers ask for a particular outcome for my loved ones, for those in need or suffering or for myself.

I wondered if God ever tires of my many requests. So I turned to the Bible. In numerous passages I received assurance that God desires my prayerful requests. Those prayers tell God of my true and abiding faith in God's grace. The apostle Paul said it well: 'Do not be anxious about anything, but in every situation, by prayer and petition, with thanksgiving, present your requests to God' (Philippians 4:6, NIV). That is exactly what I am doing today. God is love, and I am most thankful for that and for God's listening ear.

Prayer: *Dear Lord, you know what we need even before we ask. May our prayerful requests reveal our sincere and abiding faith in you. In Christ's name we pray. Amen.*

Thought for the day: Our prayerful requests profess our faith in God.

Norman A. Thomas (Virginia, USA)

Love one another

Read Colossians 3:12–17

Put away… all bitterness and wrath and anger and wrangling and slander, together with all malice. Be kind to one another, tenderhearted, forgiving one another, as God in Christ has forgiven you.
Ephesians 4:31–32 (NRSV)

My day started with hurt and irritation from a friend's critical remarks. While I ran errands my anger grew, and I began to develop a grudge. The supermarket parking lot was full, but I spotted an open space one lane over. I sped up and rounded the corner to grab it but then saw a car approaching with its blinker flashing. I scowled as I waited for the other driver to park. But to my surprise, the man stopped and waved me into the parking spot. I was grateful but unmoved by the gesture.

I raced through the store and found myself behind the same man in the check-out lane. He turned, smiled and began emptying my cart for me while the cashier scanned his items. I stood amazed. I returned the smile and thanked him for both good deeds. He shrugged and said, 'It doesn't cost anything to be nice.' I cringed and felt my face go red as I remembered Jesus' command: 'Just as I have loved you, you also should love one another' (John 13:34). I realised I was angry over something trivial, and a sudden rush of gratitude swept over me. I am thankful for the man whose acts of kindness had an impact on my attitude.

Prayer: *Dear Lord, help us to focus on being kind when things don't go our way. May we always remember to love one another no matter what the circumstances. Amen.*

Thought for the day: Showing kindness to one another can change attitudes.

Arlene Rains Graber (Kansas, USA)

God's renewing power

Read Psalm 107:33-37

He turns rivers into a desert, springs of water into thirsty ground.
Psalm 107:33 (NRSV)

One day, I looked across a valley and saw a garden of maize. I wondered why the garden had been planted in such a hot, sandy and dry place. I was surprised there could be such green growth in an almost desert area. Then I learned that the farmer had dug wells to water his garden so that he was able to plant the maize and get a plentiful harvest.

When I seem to be stuck in barren situations, God is able to make waters spring up and bring me renewed life. Oftentimes, when we feel like we are dwelling in a desert, our needs overwhelm us. When our work seems not to be yielding anything good, we feel lifeless, barren, unfruitful. But God is able and willing to cause waters to flow in the midst of our deserts to give life, fruitfulness and productivity – even where there seems to be no hope. So let us be encouraged by our powerful and loving God!

Prayer: *O Lord, may you create fruitful fields from the barren situations in our lives. In the name of Jesus. Amen.*

Thought for the day: God can bring life where there seems to be none.

Enid Adah Nyinomujuni (Dar es Salaam, Tanzania)

Making time

Read Psalm 119:97–104

Anyone who goes too far and does not continue in the teaching about Christ does not have God. Whoever continues in this teaching has both the Father and the Son.
2 John 1:9 (CEB)

At our mountain cabin, nestled among the quaking aspen, we have a small pond. Every summer a family of ducks with several ducklings nests in the pond's bulrushes, and we spend a lot of time watching them from our deck.

One day I watched as the ducklings played. Some of them explored on their own and then rushed to catch up; several scurried ahead, not waiting for their mother; and a few stayed beside the mama, mimicking her every move.

It occurred to me that their actions resembled my walk with God over the years. Many times I would lose focus, letting my Bible study and time with God take second place to more 'urgent' matters. Eventually, I would realise my need to focus on God, so I'd hurry to catch up, hoping I hadn't missed God's message for me. Other times, I would be trying to get on to the next thing, so I would rush ahead in my studies, not taking the time to meditate on scripture and its meaning. But when I have stayed anchored to God's side, following God's leading and studying scripture, I have been rewarded. Whenever I take time to hear God's voice in God's word, I find my faith is stronger and more fruitful.

Prayer: *Faithful God, help us to block out distractions and take time to walk with you, anchoring ourselves in your word. In Jesus' name. Amen.*

Thought for the day: My faith grows stronger when I make time for God and scripture.

K. L. McKee (Colorado, USA)

Behind and ahead

Read John 6:16–24

He guides me along the right paths for his name's sake.
Psalm 23:3 (NIV)

I am facing south on a long, narrow strip of land that is nearly at the southern-most point of Africa. Sometimes it is calm and beautiful at Cape Point, but today it is buffeted by storms. The raging Atlantic Ocean is on my right and the turbulent Indian Ocean to my left.

I have walked bravely but with trepidation to my present position below the towering lighthouse that has guided mariners for many years. Behind me is the solid bulk of the African continent, and far ahead of me, unseen beyond the horizon but certain in my mind, is Antarctica. I stand awed and exhilarated.

I liken my situation in this moment to my life in Christ. At times calm, at times buffeted and storm-tossed, I have walked bravely along a narrow path. Jesus is my eternal beacon. If I listen carefully I can hear his voice calming the waters and bidding me to keep the faith, knowing that behind me is the solid ground of forgiveness, power and love. Ahead of me, unseen and awesome but certain, lies eternity with Christ.

Prayer: *O God, grant us strength and guidance when we encounter the stormy gales of life. Help us to be beacons of your grace and shelter for others. In Jesus' name we pray. Amen.*

Thought for the day: I will trust Christ to guide me along God's path.

Keith Honeyman (Western Cape, South Africa)

The vase

Read 1 John 1:5–10

If we confess our sins, he is faithful and just and will forgive our sins and purify us from all unrighteousness.
1 John 1:9 (NIV)

The glass vase was positioned on the dusty shelf at the back of the workshop. I decided it was the ideal present I was seeking and presented it at the counter. The glassblower offered to clean it before wrapping it, but I didn't want her to bother and hold up the queue; I'd wash it later. No, she insisted, the vase wasn't leaving her workshop in a dirty condition. She disappeared and returned with a gleaming, sparkling ornament. It looked like a jewel! It was stunning! Clean and polished, the light brought out all the beauty of the rich design. She was rightly proud of her work and wanted it to be enjoyed in its full splendour.

But I left the workshop challenged. I thought of my relationship with God and of the times I want to ignore my sin, failures and shortcomings or am just not bothered to bring them to God for cleansing. Likewise with the hurts and pain which I keep hold of and which weigh me down.

How much I need God's forgiveness. God's sole desire is to cleanse and heal, to pour his grace and love right into the depths of my life. God's forgiveness and love and beauty can only shine out of me when I put myself into his hands to be made clean.

Prayer: *Lord Jesus, we confess our need of your deep cleaning today. Forgive us, heal us and pour your power within. Amen.*

Thought for the day: God's grace *is* sufficient.

Hilary Allen (England, United Kingdom)

God's comfort

Read Isaiah 66:7–13

'As a mother comforts her child, so will I comfort you.'
Isaiah 66:13 (NIV)

One dark, frosty morning my mother called and asked me to come help her and my father because she was experiencing dizziness and vomiting. When I heard her feeble voice, my stomach turned into a knot, my hands started sweating, and I felt my heartbeat in my throat. I had lost my husband the year before and had experienced multiple difficult life changes, so I was already feeling vulnerable and distressed. I thought, *God, my life is hard enough without having to handle one more crisis.* I felt as if God had abandoned me.

When I came home after an exhausting day with my parents, I opened my Bible. God spoke to me through Isaiah 66:13. In this chapter, the Lord spoke to the Israelites, ensuring them that God had not abandoned them and offering them comfort and hope for the restoration of Jerusalem.

God longs to comfort us. In our most difficult moments, God whispers words of peace, love, comfort and encouragement to our souls. When I was deeply distressed, God brought comfort to my heart, heard my prayers and gave me strength to help my parents. Our good God desires our well-being and is ready to extend comfort and peace anytime.

Prayer: *Dear Lord, we come to you, asking for your comfort and peace. Comfort us as a mother comforts her child. Ease our pain and fill our hearts with encouragement. Amen.*

Thought for the day: I will ask for and receive God's comfort today.

Hadassah Treu (Pazardzhik, Bulgaria)

PRAYER FOCUS: TO FEEL GOD'S COMFORT

God's protection

Read Psalm 57

Have mercy on me, my God, have mercy on me, for in you I take refuge. I will take refuge in the shadow of your wings until the disaster has passed.
Psalm 57:1 (NIV)

My wife and I operate a small farm. One evening, we were away from home when we received a call from our neighbour who told us that one of our cows was having her calf in the pasture. The time immediately after birth can be dangerous for both the mother and the newborn since both are weak and the birth process often attracts predators.

It was dark when we got home. After getting our flashlights and going out to the pasture, we were rewarded with the sight of a healthy newborn calf lying beside its mother. We also found our llamas and guard dog standing in a circle around the cow and calf. The llamas and dog provided comfort and protection to their vulnerable charges. As we moved the cow and her calf to the barn, we were escorted by the llamas and dog.

For me, that was a memorable illustration of the protection and refuge that God provides. We may not face the same physical threats as livestock, but we do face fear, worry, temptation, loneliness and grief that prey on our relationship with God. When I look back at difficult times in my life, I can see that God provided protection and comfort, often in the form of support from fellow Christians. Just as the llamas and dog provided protection and comfort to the cow and her calf, God provides protection and comfort to us.

Prayer: *Our Father, thank you for the many ways you comfort us when we are vulnerable. Help us always to find our refuge in you. Amen.*

Thought for the day: God is my refuge, especially when I am the most vulnerable.

David Anglen (Texas, USA)

Giving it to God

Read Philippians 4:10–13

I am not saying this because I am in need, for I have learned to be content whatever the circumstances.
Philippians 4:11 (NIV)

After I learned that I had torn my other ACL, my spirits sank. I had just recovered from the same injury to my other knee eight months prior, and now I was going to have to go through the same gruelling journey all over again. Surgery, crutches, ice and physical therapy would be my main focus for the next two weeks. I felt as if I would never understand where God was in all this or how God could possibly use this injury for my good.

It was around this time that I came across Philippians 4. I was familiar with this passage of scripture, but I had never spent much time studying and meditating on it. After reading it, I decided that although I did not understand why I was going through this trial, I knew that turning to God would be the only way I could get through it. I took a leap of faith and decided to trust God. Now I have found joy and a peace that I did not have when I was healing from my first knee injury. Giving this struggle to God is something I have to do every day, and doing so helps me remember that I am not going through this hardship alone.

Prayer: *Dear God, help us give our struggles to you daily, and remind us that the trials that we go through will strengthen our faith and trust in you. Amen.*

Thought for the day: I do not have to go through any struggle alone because God goes with me.

Courtney Canion (Texas, USA)

A fruitful vine

Read John 15:1–8

'I am the vine; you are the branches. If you remain in me and I in you, you will bear much fruit; apart from me you can do nothing.'
John 15:5 (NIV)

One sunny morning I woke up to the sound of birds chirping. I looked out my window and saw that it was the long tendrils of my passion fruit plant that had attracted the birds. I recalled Jesus' words in John 15:5 and meditated on the verse with curiosity, knowing that the Holy Spirit had brought it to my mind to reveal something to me.

I realised that the image of the vine in John 15:5 and my passion fruit plant have something in common – they both have winding, clinging branches that bear fruit. They don't have trunks; they cling to nearby objects for support and their branches grow out of the vine. In John 15:5, Jesus was making it clear to us that he supplies our needs and makes it possible for us to flourish.

In order to thrive and bear fruit, climbing plants depend on a strong central vine and require occasional pruning. Jesus is our true vine, and when we remain connected to him, we can bear much fruit. All we need to do is receive and rest in Jesus' love. Just as a plant's nutrients flow from the vine to its branches, God's divine love flows from Christ to us.

Prayer: *Dear Lord, as we cling to you, restore our peace and hope and remind us how much you love us. Amen.*

Thought for the day: Through nature, I can learn about God.

Joshua Sila (Nairobi, Kenya)

Letting go

Read Matthew 11:28–30

The Lord is close to the broken-hearted and saves those who are crushed in spirit.
Psalm 34:18 (NIV)

My family had experienced three recent deaths: my father, my mother and my nephew. After cleaning out my parents' house for a new family to move in, reality hit hard. We would never gather at my childhood home again. Dad would not read Luke 2 on Christmas Day. Mum would not make raspberry jelly or pecan pies. My nephew would not give another prank gift or bear hug. Our family would never be the same.

As I walked through the empty house, Dad's orchard and the woods at the edge of the yard, I cried. I thanked God for a great family and childhood home and asked for God's blessings on the young family who would live here now. Yet, a few hours later, I realised I had never given God my grief. I understood in a new way that God loves us and reaches out to us in our sorrow. However, we must offer our sorrow and grief to God.

Doing so does not remove our pain or eliminate the need for grieving. But it does offer the assurance that God holds our lives and sustains us through any devastating loss. We will never have to carry our burdens alone because God carries them with us.

Prayer: *Thank you, never-failing Father, for your presence, comfort and peace, especially in times of grief. Amen.*

Thought for the day: I find comfort and reassurance when I offer my burdens to God.

Diana Derringer (Kentucky, USA)

PRAYER FOCUS: THOSE GRIEVING A LOSS

Moving on

Read Judges 6:33–40

The Lord said to Abram, 'Leave your land, your family, and your father's household for the land that I will show you.'
Genesis 12:1 (CEB)

As I have gotten older, I have felt more resistant to change. So when I felt God asking me to make a major life change – moving to live in a city on the other side of my country where I knew no one – I didn't want to go. It would mean leaving behind my friends and my church. But while I continued to disobey this urging, I had no peace.

I tried to calm my unsettled soul by reading about characters in the Bible who had been asked to move by God. Abram was prompted by God to move to an unknown destination; at least I knew where God wanted me to go. God asked David to change his location and his status; I would only be changing my location. Gideon was so reluctant to obey that he questioned God and tested God's intentions with a fleece; I didn't need a fleece.

I obeyed God's instructions questioningly and reluctantly. I am now living in a house that is better suited to my older age. I am happy in my new church, and since moving I have learned that my former church has closed. The city I now live in has more opportunities for service. I will be forever grateful God urged me to move. God always knows best.

Prayer: *Dear God, may we always obey your still, small voice. Give us courage to follow your leading. Amen.*

Thought for the day: God knows what is best for me.

Carol Purves (England, United Kingdom)

The finest wine

Read John 2:1–11
Remain in me as I also remain in you.
John 15:4 (NIV)

On holiday in Cornwall I visited a vineyard. It was fascinating to learn about the vines and soil and how the weather conditions, by affecting the sugar content of the grapes, have such an important influence on the wine that is produced. How amazing that the same wine from three consecutive years can taste entirely different.

I thought a lot about the miracle that Jesus performed at Cana, changing water into wine. To save an embarassing situation at a wedding, whereby the wine had run out, his mother Mary asked Jesus to intervene. As the guests had already had plenty to drink, any wine would have been acceptable. Instead, Jesus transformed the water – hundreds of litres of it – into the best wine that the master of the banquet had tasted.

Similarly, on the day of Pentecost, the coming of the Holy Spirit transformed Jesus' disciples, empowering them to be used by God in ways they could never have imagined. Indeed, the transformation was such that people thought they had drunk too much wine (see Acts 2:13)!

Do you want your life to be transformed? Just as in the Lord's hands water can be turned into the finest wine, so can we be changed in extraordinary ways by the empowering presence of Jesus, the true vine.

Prayer: *Lord, we want your Spirit to be at work in us, so that we are empowered to do your will. Amen.*

Thought for the day: I will remain in Jesus.

Ann Armstrong (England, United Kingdom)

Finding joy

Read John 2:1–11

You changed my mourning into dancing. You took off my funeral clothes and dressed me up in joy so that my whole being might sing praises to you and never stop.
Psalm 30:11–12 (CEB)

A few years ago, I felt uncomfortable in the workplace due to the attitudes and actions of my boss and some colleagues. The situation got so bad I was at the point of quitting my job.

I started to read the Bible and *The Upper Room* daily devotional meditations and gave my life to Christ. I read other people's stories of situations like mine in the daily meditations. I learned I was not the only person going through difficult times. But God speaks to each of us in different ways. I learned to pray, first giving thanks to God for all things and then turning my concerns over to God.

Today, my boss is no longer with the company, the working relationship with my colleagues has changed and I have received recognition for my years of service. What I know for sure is that God never abandons us and can change our mourning into dancing.

Prayer: *Blessed be your name, O Lord. Thank you for helping us find joy and peace in the many blessings we receive every day. We pray as you taught us, 'Father, hallowed be your name, your kingdom come. Give us each day our daily bread. Forgive us our sins, for we also forgive everyone who sins against us. And lead us not into temptation'* (Luke 11:2–4, NIV). Amen.

Thought for the day: God will never leave me.

Daniel Valencia Guevara (State of Mexico, Mexico)

Good gifts

Read Matthew 7:7–12

If you, then, though you are evil, know how to give good gifts to your children, how much more will your Father in heaven give good gifts to those who ask him!
Matthew 7:11 (NIV)

Three-year-old Kate had spent a day with me the previous week, and she delighted in the strawberries I had given her as a snack. When I picked her up again, her first words to me were, 'Do you have strawberries?' I told her I didn't, and I watched her eyes cloud and her smile fade. I quickly added, 'But I do have oranges and bananas.' Kate's eyes brightened, and she excitedly exclaimed, 'Yeah, I like those too!' Kate enjoyed the oranges and bananas as much as she had enjoyed the strawberries.

This sweet interaction with Kate made me ponder our responses to God. We often ask for blessings and hope to receive the same gifts we were given before. But God may have a different gift in store for us. Do we respond positively to God's good gift or do we wish for something else?

When we pray, we should be open to the gifts that God has for us in the present. James tells us, 'Every good and perfect gift is from above, coming down from the Father of the heavenly lights' (James 1:17). God has a variety of gifts and blessings to offer, and each one may be different than the last. We can anticipate them all with the excitement and joy of a child.

Prayer: *Loving Father, thank you for the many gifts you have given us in the past. Help us to be open to the good gifts you are giving us today. Amen.*

Thought for the day: God has good gifts for me today!

Jamie Fugitt (Missouri, USA)

God's beautiful world

Read Psalm 95:1–7

The flowers appear on the earth; the time of singing has come, and the voice of the turtledove is heard in our land.
Song of Songs 2:12 (NRSV)

I've always wished I could have some plants in my mobile home, but I never seem to have the energy or the ability to make that happen. A few weeks ago, however, a friend gave me a beautiful coleus plant in a small pot. The leaves were magenta, and the plant brightened the window area of my living room.

Later my friend came to visit and said the plant needed to be trimmed. As he trimmed it, he handed me two of the small leaf sections he had cut off. He said that if I put them in a glass of water, they would form roots, and then I could plant them. After a week or so I looked at the glass; to my astonishment, new roots filled it! I planted them in potting soil, and now I have three beautiful coleus plants that are growing vigorously.

My experience with these plants made me think of the beauty God has placed all around us. Who can doubt God's creation when such wonders abound! Genesis 1:12 tells of the beginning of God's creative beauty: 'And God saw that it was good.' And Jesus said, 'Even Solomon in all his glory was not clothed like one of these' (Luke 12:27).

God created the world with boundless beauty. Such beauty reminds us that God is present and will care for us all our days.

Prayer: *Dear Lord, help us not to neglect seeing the beauty in your creation. In the name of Jesus, the Lily of the Valley. Amen.*

Thought for the day: God makes all things beautiful.

Ken Claar (Idaho, USA)

Lost and found

Read Luke 15:11–32

This thy brother was dead, and is alive again; and was lost, and is found.
Luke 15:32 (KJV)

As I grow older, I am more inclined to forget where I have put things. So I have developed the habit of asking God to help me find what I have lost, and God graciously responds.

In Luke 15, we read of a lost coin, a lost sheep and a lost son. Each was precious to the one who had suffered the loss, and great was the rejoicing when the lost was found.

Many people have lost something that they think they will never find: a reputation, innocence, faith, hope, joy, enthusiasm, vision, purpose. Many have lost their first love for God. But when Jesus told these stories, he was offering hope for restoration.

Yes, God is kind and helps us with everyday situations – like lost household items. But God is greatly concerned about people who are lost – those who have drifted away or who have never been close to begin with. God longs to bring all of us home and restore us. When we have lost our way in the struggles of life, we can come to God and pour our heart out to our loving Father. God will always welcome us, embrace us, love us and restore us.

Prayer: *Dear God, may the love you show us through others lead us back to you. Amen.*

Thought for the day: When I feel lost, I can turn to God, who will always welcome me home.

Valerie Clark (KwaZulu-Natal, South Africa)

Always present

Read Deuteronomy 31:3–8

'I, Jesus, have sent my angel to give you this testimony for the churches. I am the Root and the Offspring of David, and the bright Morning Star.'

Revelation 22:16 (NIV)

It had been raining steadily for five days, and the local forecast was predicting another two days of equally bleak conditions. I found myself increasingly unmotivated to do much of anything, especially when it involved going outside. Taking out the trash, driving to work, letting the dog out – everything was a wet, depressing chore that sapped my energy and dampened my disposition.

Having not seen the sun in nearly a week, I decided to head to the gym in hopes that some physical activity might change my outlook. While driving through a particularly strong downpour, the rain suddenly stopped, the clouds broke and the sun shone through long enough to change my perspective. In that moment, I was able to recognise that, though it had been shrouded by the storm, the sun was never gone. So it is with God, who will always be with us, never leaving or forsaking us.

Too often, we are so focused on worldly cares that we forget that, even in the midst of our storms, Jesus is still 'the bright Morning Star'. It is good to remember that clouds cannot stop the light of the sun; they can only obscure it for a time. Similarly, Christ never leaves us. He is with us through it all, ordering our days and preparing straight paths for when the clouds lift.

Prayer: *Thank you, God, for your faithfulness every day, no matter the storm surrounding us. Amen.*

Thought for the day: When things seem dark, the light of Christ still shines.

Todd Noon (New Jersey, USA)

Framed in worry

Read Psalm 46:1–3

God is our refuge and strength, an ever-present help in trouble.
Psalm 46:1 (NIV)

I woke up one morning full of worries. *How is my daughter-in-law managing with the children; are they sick? Can I make my meeting this afternoon? Will I have time to pick up groceries?* All this worry and I still had not risen from my bed! My day was framed in worry.

As I read my Bible, I felt my mood lighten and an optimistic spirit settle into my heart and mind. Psalm 46:1–2 says: 'God is our refuge and our strength, an ever-present help in trouble. Therefore we will not fear, though the earth give way and the mountains fall into the heart of the sea.' What an unshakeable peace and confidence in the face of momentous events! This psalm gives strength and courage for the coming day.

When we choose trust rather than worry, our day will be marked by confidence, assurance and strength. The important tasks will be done, and we will finish the day satisfied. At the end of the day we will be able to lay our heads on our pillow and sleep in peace. As Psalm 4:8 assures us: 'In peace I will lie down and sleep.' With the help of God's word, let us frame our days not with worry but with peace.

Prayer: *Dear Lord, thank you for caring for us and giving us the strength to face all of the worries each day brings. Help us to frame each day with your peace. Amen.*

Thought for the day: I will choose to begin each day by placing my trust in God.

Brenda Lee Birch (Alberta, Canada)

PRAYER FOCUS: THOSE EXPERIENCING ANXIETY

It's all in the family

Read 1 John 3:11–18

I kneel before the Father, from whom every family in heaven and on earth derives its name.
Ephesians 3:14–15 (NIV)

I hate to admit it, but my children and grandchildren are not perfect. But even though I may not always agree with or approve of their actions, I will forever love them unconditionally. I consider myself a tolerant person, but I don't appreciate it when others want to harm or criticise my family. In those times, I will speak up even though I'm timid.

Because of the intense love I feel for my family, I think I have a small understanding of God's love for all of us, God's children. None of us is perfect, but we are all God's creation. When I want to be critical or judgemental of others, I try to remind myself that I would not appreciate hateful remarks about my own family. I need to give the same respect to God's children.

Furthermore, as a parent and grandparent, nothing thrills me more than when others recognise the goodness of my family and give them support and affection. As imperfect as we all are, I believe God is truly pleased when we see and appreciate the good in God's children.

Prayer: *Dear Father, thank you for loving us all as your children. We pray that you will guide us to love all your children as you have loved us. Amen.*

Thought for the day: God can lead me to recognise the good in others.

Ruth Gunter Mitchell (Alabama, USA)

Birds of the air

Read Matthew 6:25–34

'Look at the birds of the air; they do not sow or reap or store away in barns, and yet your heavenly Father feeds them. Are you not much more valuable than they? Can any one of you by worrying add a single hour to your life?'
Matthew 6:26–27 (NIV)

It was Monday morning, and I was tired and sad. The past few weeks had been busy with work and travel. The anniversary of the death of my soulmate was fast approaching, and I had been thinking about her a lot. I had spent the weekend with my kids, and my heart was breaking for them in the loss of their mother.

The Upper Room devotion that morning was about listening to God. As hard as I tried, I could not sit still and listen. I prayed for my kids, got another cup of coffee and sat down in my living room. As I sat down, a bird perched on my front door rail just outside the living room window. I immediately knew that God was speaking to me even though I was not listening.

Seeing that bird reminded me of the sermon on the mount, where Jesus teaches us about worry. He tells us that God takes care of the birds in the sky and that we are more important than the birds. As I pondered the scripture and its meaning, I began to appreciate some things I had taken for granted. I felt God giving me much-needed inner strength. I appreciated the message God sent to me in a time when I most needed it.

Prayer: *Thank you, God, for speaking to us when we most need it. Help us to listen for your voice. Amen.*

Thought for the day: How am I listening for God's voice today?

Steve Wakefield (Alabama, USA)

Inspired to write

Read Psalm 139:13–18

I praise you because I am fearfully and wonderfully made.
Psalm 139:14 (NIV)

When I arrived home from painting class, I checked my email. My mood plummeted when I found that my devotional submission had been rejected. I reviewed the list of possible reasons for the rejection that the publisher sent. Then I read my meditation several times, trying to discern why it wasn't accepted.

For aspiring writers, rejections are discouraging. Sometimes rejected meditations cause me to doubt my God-given purpose. But still I labour at my craft. My heart's desire is to glorify God through my writing and to share my faith experiences with others.

But writing is hard work. It requires discipline and commitment, as well as a teachable spirit. Rejections, though discouraging, are also a catalyst for continued learning and practice. So when discouragement threatens to derail my efforts, I recall today's quoted verse and remember why I write: It's an expression of my love for others and for God. Whether or not my meditations are published, God is pleased with my efforts. When God weaves within us a divine purpose, God also equips us to persevere. And so as my words flow across the page, I continue to answer God's call on my life.

Prayer: *Heavenly Father, help us remain committed when we face rejection. Give us teachable spirits and the will to persevere in our response to your call. Amen.*

Thought for the day: I will persevere in the purpose God has given me.

Debra Pierce (Massachusetts, USA)

Prompting from God

Read 1 Corinthians 2:6–16

Who knows a person's thoughts except their own spirit within them? In the same way no one knows the thoughts of God except the Spirit of God.

1 Corinthians 2:11 (NIV)

I had kept a Bible in the backseat of my car for several weeks with the belief that God would show me whom to give it to at the right moment. When I arrived at work one morning and got out of my car, I felt a conviction and a nudge from God that I should take the Bible inside with me.

That morning, one of my coworkers looked sad and subdued. She told me that her dad was being tested for a serious illness and explained her fears about his possible diagnosis. Feeling certain this was the reason God had prompted me to bring the Bible inside, I took it out of my bag and told her about my belief. She hugged me, thanking me with tears in her eyes. I told her it was not my merit; I was only an instrument in God's hands.

I prayed for my coworker's dad. Ultimately, the test results showed that the doctor's concerns about possible serious illness had been wrong. My coworker now looks to the future with confidence, and she places her hope in God. Every day we try to find time at work for a little break with God.

Prayer: *Dear God, thank you for listening to our prayers, for opening our hearts, for helping us to give joyfully to others and for giving us clear convictions and guidance. Amen.*

Thought for the day: When I listen to God's promptings, I can make a difference for others.

Jolanta Burzynska (Warmia-Masuria, Poland)

Given for you

Read Luke 18:15–17

'Let the little children come to me, and do not hinder them, for the kingdom of God belongs to such as these.'
Luke 18:16 (NIV)

It was an exciting Sunday for my daughter Petra. She would be receiving Communion for the first time at our new church.

Petra was excited. Finally our turn came to receive the elements. When Petra stood in front of the pastor he instinctively placed his hand on her head and offered the children's blessing, forgetting that she was supposed to receive Communion that Sunday. As she turned to walk back to our pew I could see the crestfallen look on Petra's face. 'It's okay,' I said, 'he just forgot.' 'I know, Dad. It's fine.' But I could see that it wasn't.

But then, as the pastor was covering the Communion elements, he took one wafer and one small cup and began walking down the aisle towards the back of the church. He made his way to the middle of the row where Petra was sitting and spoke the words, 'The body of Christ broken for you, the blood of Christ, shed for you.' That experience remains for me a powerful and tender reminder that Jesus comes to each of us. We are not forgotten.

Prayer: *Inviting God, we are grateful that you come to each of us with signs that we belong to you. Amen.*

Thought for the day: God sees me; I am not forgotten.

Pete Velander (Tennessee, USA)

Restored

Read Psalm 56

But now, Lord, you are our father. We are the clay, and you are our potter. All of us are the work of your hand.
Isaiah 64:8 (CEB)

Some time ago, I experienced several life changes. I resigned from my job to move several times because of my husband's work. During one of those moves, I was led by God to be baptised. Six months after I was baptised, my husband and I went through a hard time; my marriage was in crisis. He talked about a separation and later asked that I leave the house. At the same time this was happening, my grandmother, who had been like a mother to me during my youth, died. Two months later, my father died.

Unable to understand what was happening, I was filled with incredible suffering and my heart was broken. I fell to my knees and asked God, 'Why did you take everything?' I entered a prolonged season of prayer and fasting. With anguished urgency I began to read the Bible and the Holy Spirit led me to this passage: 'Record my misery; list my tears on your scroll – are they not in your record? Then my enemies will turn back when I call for help. By this I will know that God is for me' (Psalm 56:8–9, NIV). An inexplicable peace washed over me. My life, the vessel that was broken into pieces, could be made new again. God was at work sustaining, moulding and refining the fragments of my heart. This process not only restored my life but my marriage as well and filled me with God's peace.

Prayer: *Dear Lord, grant us the wisdom to trust you to mould and remake us according to your will. Amen.*

Thought for the day: In the hands of the potter, I am restored to new life.

Evelyn G. Figueroa (Puerto Rico)

Pass it on

Read Psalm 12:41–44

Calling his disciples to him, Jesus said, 'Truly I tell you, this poor widow has put more into the treasury than all the others.'
Mark 12:43 (NIV)

Several years ago, while we were acclimating to a new church, a kind member began the habit of passing a copy of *The Upper Room* to our family. At the time, our children were in school and our lives seemed very full. We wondered how we would find the time each day to gather the family together to accomplish yet one more task. We began to set aside a few minutes each morning after breakfast before our day got too busy and our children headed off to school. Before long, we had gotten into a wonderful routine! Occasionally, something would interfere with it, and the morning devotional would be overlooked. It didn't take us long to make a connection that the days begun with devotionals went more smoothly than the ones without.

Decades later we are still beginning our days with *The Upper Room* at breakfast, and we have started the tradition of 'passing on' the devotional to friends and family members, just as our friend had done for us. Over the years, our lives have been enriched by the messages of spirit-filled Christians from all over the globe. It all began with a humble act of sharing Christ's love.

Prayer: *Help us, Lord, to pass on to others the generous gifts of love you have given to us. Amen.*

Thought for the day: Acts of kindness are generous gifts of God's love.

Diana Clark (Rhode Island, USA)

A new life

Read Psalm 8

Yea, though I walk through the valley of the shadow of death, I will fear no evil: for thou art with me; thy rod and thy staff they comfort me.
Psalm 23:4 (KJV)

At 11.30 am on 28 December 2021, I suddenly started sweating, and I knew that I needed to go to the hospital. My family members called my eldest son who was on duty at the hospital to come pick me up. At that time, hospitals were crowded, and it was difficult to see doctors there, but I met with a capable doctor who diagnosed me with two blockages in my heart. We made an immediate decision to perform an angioplasty and open the blockages with two stents.

The surgery was successful. I was kept in the ICU for one day and in a special observation room for another. On the evening of the third day, I returned home completely recovered. I am convinced that the living God gave me a new life.

The life I am leading today is a living witness to the words of the psalmist: 'Though I walk through the valley of the shadow of death, I will fear no evil: for thou art with me.' Through my experience that day, I have seen the full promise of the Lord, who stayed with me all the time and walked with me through the valley. I thank the Lord for giving me new life.

Prayer: *Merciful God, increase our faith. Help us to believe that you are ready to take care of us and help us when we pray to you. In the name of the Lord Jesus. Amen.*

Thought for the day: God walks with me through every valley.

Jaiprakash D. Roy (Gujarat, India)

Sticky-note prayers

Read Ephesians 6:17–20

Pray in the Spirit on all occasions with all kinds of prayers and requests.
Ephesians 6:18 (NIV)

After my husband and I married, we had conflicting schedules. I was working on my bachelor's degree, and he often worked evening shifts as a meteorologist. I came home one afternoon to find a note taped to the fireplace. We began communicating via these short notes when our schedules didn't line up. We stuck them on the bathroom mirror, the door to the garage, in the kitchen and in other places where they were sure to attract attention. My son didn't understand our history with the notes and disliked them, but my husband and I knew they were love notes with the intent of maintaining communication.

Like those notes, our prayers don't have to be long-winded. Short prayers throughout the day strengthen our relationship with God. The apostle Paul tells us to 'rejoice always, pray without ceasing, give thanks in all circumstances' (1 Thessalonians 5:16–18, NRSV). This means not just praising God for the things we are happy about, but also for things that might not give us joy. Rejoicing, praising, praying and thanking God are all ways we can include God in our day, and I believe it is a wonderful way to honour God.

Prayer: *Dear Lord, thank you for hearing even our shortest prayers. Help us remember that nothing is too trivial to pray about. In the name of Jesus, we pray. Amen.*

Thought for the day: I honour God with my praise, prayers and thankfulness each day.

Mary Hunt Webb (New Mexico, USA)

Spiritual growth

Read Leviticus 6:8–13

The fire must be kept burning on the altar continuously; it must not go out.

Leviticus 6:13 (NIV)

In my sister's garden, spinach blossomed with irresistible green leaves and lush shoots. I wanted to replicate this sight at my house, so I picked some seedlings for my small garden. Weeks passed, but my spinach did not produce the same beauty. I studied my sister's method, and I realised I had missed an important step. Every morning before going to work, she waters the garden with water from her small fishpond, providing the plants with daily nutrients and making her garden green and lush.

The Holy Spirit taught me a great lesson from this observation. At that time, I had not applied the principle of daily nurture to my Christian faith. I woke early to beat the traffic on my way to work. If I was running late, I would skip my morning devotion or say my prayers in a hurry. Some days got so busy that I had no time to return to my devotions. This inconsistent care for my faith was precarious.

Just like the daily addition of wood kept the fire on the altar burning in Leviticus 6:12–13, the daily care my sister gives her plants keeps her garden green. To get the same result in my spiritual life, I must pray and meditate on God's word every day. Those who blossom spiritually do not get there by chance; they consistently work at it. This is the recipe for spiritual growth.

Prayer: *Dear Lord, forgive us when we are too busy to give attention to you. Help us to prioritise our spiritual growth by spending time with you each day. Amen.*

Thought for the day: How will I create time for fellowship with God?

Muyiwa Benralph Olaiya (Federal Capital Territory, Nigeria)

In awe

Read Psalm 19

The heavens declare the glory of God; the skies proclaim the work of his hands.
Psalm 19:1 (NIV)

I recently went camping with friends. As I sat in front of the campfire, my legs warm and aglow from the flames, I looked up at the array of stars speckling the night sky. Having been in the city for a long time, I hadn't seen stars so clearly in years. It pulled me back to the many memories I have of sitting under the stars and feeling the vastness of creation. And like the writer of Psalm 19, I knew in that moment that God was good because I was experiencing the goodness of God's handiwork.

All weekend as we hiked, swam and enjoyed the outdoors, I could sense the fine detail God has woven into creation. I remembered how nature affects our entire being and involves all our senses. I think God made nature all-encompassing so that it would command our attention. Psalm 19:4–6 talks about how the sun's heat affects every part of the earth as it circles the sky. In the same way, God's love affects every part of us as we remain in God.

Prayer: *Dear God, thank you for the goodness of your creation. Help us to remember that the beauty of your creation is a reflection of your love for us. Amen.*

Thought for the day: I can experience God's goodness through the world around me.

Avery Ochs (Texas, USA)

A bird in the storm

Read Luke 12:22–34

'Be strong and courageous. Do not be afraid… for the Lord your God goes with you; he will never leave you nor forsake you.'
Deuteronomy 31:6 (NIV)

My wife and I sat in our sunroom and watched a storm rage outside. As we watched the rain pour down and heard the thunder rumble, we noticed a purple martin flying through the wind and rain. She flew up to her nest under the eaves at the corner of our house. We could hear the chirping of her babies as she brought them a tiny insect, and then with a chirp of her own, she took off to find more for them to eat. Time after time she returned and then took off again. The heavy rain and strong wind occasionally blew her off course, but she never stopped. Our admiration for her grew with each trip she made, and we both remarked that there was something inspirational about her behaviour.

Long after the storm ended, I kept thinking about what we had witnessed. The mother bird's behaviour made me think of the sacrifice that Jesus made for all of us. Like the purple martin, his sacrifice was an act of intense love! The little bird's determined care for her young reminded us that God really does care about and provide for all of creation. God's love will endure and will not be turned aside by the storms of adversity. I pray that the devotion of the little bird will stay alive in my memory and inspire me to show love to others and to trust God.

Prayer: *Dear Jesus, thank you for the sacrifice you made for us so that we may live abundantly. Inspire us to show your love to the world. Amen.*

Thought for the day: Reminders of God's enduring love are all around me.

Jack L. Bodden (Texas, USA)

Trust in God

Read Psalm 18:1–6

In my distress I called to the Lord; I cried to my God for help. From his temple he heard my voice; my cry came before him, into his ears.
Psalm 18:6 (NIV)

My life has been a wreck for the past three years. In 2018, my contract came to an end at the power station where I worked, and I was unemployed. In 2019 I started to put my life together by doing ad-hoc training in schools. Soon after, the country was placed under lockdown due to the Covid-19 pandemic, and everything came to a standstill.

My wife continued with her sewing business making face masks, and she was able to keep the family going. But on 25 December 2020, my wife and friend of 38 years, the breadwinner for our family, passed away. I felt my life was over. The future looked bleak. However, during all this adversity, not a single day went by without food or other daily necessities being provided for me, my two children and my granddaughter. God has carried us thus far.

No matter what we are going through, God hears our prayers. When we find ourselves wrecked by life's troubles, when we feel hopeless and overwhelmed, we may not be able to hear God, but God can hear us. God hears our cries of pain and desperation and offers comfort and encouragement to help us endure.

Prayer: *Heavenly Father, give us strength to endure our pain and sorrow. Give us courage, and reassure us of your constant love and care. Amen.*

Thought for the day: When I am afraid, I will put my trust in God.

David Kgabodiso (Gauteng, South Africa)

The better part

Read Luke 10:38–42

The Lord answered her, 'Martha, Martha, you are worried and distracted by many things, but few things are needed – indeed only one. Mary has chosen the better part, which will not be taken away from her.'
Luke 10:41–42 (NRSV)

After being diagnosed with multiple sclerosis in December 2016, I was unable to carry out my usual physical activities on many days. I have neuropathy from the ribs down, debilitating fatigue, muscle spasms and pain. For a while I felt useless and lonely. I wondered if my best days were behind me.

Then I read the story of Mary and Martha. Martha was frustrated that Mary wasn't helping her with the preparations for hosting Jesus and his disciples in their home. Jesus calmed Martha, saying that Mary was exactly where she needed to be – with him. That scripture helped me to see that even in times of incapacity, I could still be useful – even productive. I began to relinquish control and began sitting at the feet of Jesus, loving him and feeling loved by him. While I was incapacitated, God helped me to grow in my faith by leading me to read my Bible and to engage in other devotional activities.

In the years since my diagnosis, I have found a way to continue working full-time at the local community college. I'm also able to foster dogs and volunteer with several local fundraising events. I am comforted to know that Jesus is always with me and can use me at all times to serve him, no matter my physical capabilities.

Prayer: *Lord Jesus, comfort us with your love when we feel useless or alone. Thank you for walking beside us. Amen.*

Thought for the day: Who do I need to be today – Mary or Martha?

Patsy D. Fields (South Carolina, USA)

Out of my comfort zone

Read Psalm 23

'I came that they may have life and have it abundantly.'
John 10:10 (NRSV)

Many years ago, I was asked to go on a mission trip abroad. I declined because of numerous conflicts – family activities, work demands and other commitments. I thought the next trip would fit my schedule better. But after a few more years and opportunities, I still had not participated.

Then in 2005, I was invited to go on a mission trip to Guatemala. Even though many of the same conflicts existed, I felt God nudging me to go. As I prayed about the opportunity, I realised that my conflicts were really excuses to avoid stepping out of my comfort zone.

I did go on that trip, followed by seven more trips over the next eight years. As we offered our help to those we encountered, I also gained a better perspective on the meaning of 'abundant life.' The people we met possessed joy, peace and love for God – the abundant life – that made a lasting impression on me.

That first trip was a small investment of time, but a big step in my walk of faith because I was willing to leave the familiar and move forward in faith trusting God.

Prayer: *God of second chances, open our hearts so that we will be ready to respond to your call. Help us to be obedient to you, to discern your will for our lives and to go forward in faith. Amen.*

Thought for the day: God provides many opportunities for me to say yes.

John D. Bown (Minnesota, USA)

The wonders of God

Read Genesis 1:1–28

Before the mountains were born, before you birthed the earth and the inhabited world – from forever in the past to forever in the future, you are God.
Psalm 90:2 (CEB)

A few years ago, to mitigate the pain of losing my father, I took up painting classes at my church. I did it as a diversion, really. But God knows exactly why and how such circumstances work to benefit our lives.

When I started painting, I learned to take a closer look at all of creation. What joy! I was in awe of the majestic mountains, flowing rivers and robust forests. Added to this joy was taking a painting class with wonderful people in a setting of fellowship and friendship.

God created all the wonders that surround us and placed them in our care for us to enjoy. As children of God, it is most fitting to praise the creator with grateful hearts.

Prayer: *Creator of heaven and earth, we praise you for your immense generosity to place all your creation under our stewardship. Teach us to be more grateful and to fulfil our commitment to care for all you have entrusted to us as we pray: 'Our Father which art in heaven, Hallowed be thy name. Thy kingdom come. Thy will be done, as in heaven, so in earth. Give us day by day our daily bread. And forgive us our sins; for we also forgive every one that is indebted to us. And lead us not into temptation; but deliver us from evil' (Luke 11:2–4, KJV). Amen.*

Thought for the day: God's creation is our delight and our responsibility.

María Cristina Olivares Guzmán (Bogotá, Colombia)

Ash Wednesday

Read Matthew 6:9–15

If you forgive other people when they sin against you, your heavenly Father will also forgive you.
Matthew 6:14 (NIV)

I had never given up anything for Lent because the practice did not seem meaningful to me. Then one year on Ash Wednesday, my pastor challenged us to think differently about giving up something for Lent. He asked us to think of a person we were holding a grudge or anger or resentment against and invited us to forgive them.

Years earlier I had gone through a divorce. My spouse had cheated on me again and again. I had been so deeply hurt. How could I ever forgive him? I struggled with my feelings. Was I ready to release all the pain he had caused me? Finally I decided, that yes, I was going to forgive.

The pastor asked us to write on a piece of paper what we were giving up. I wrote it down, then folded the piece of paper. The congregation was then invited to burn our slips of paper in a bowl. It was one of the most meaningful Ash Wednesday services I had ever attended.

It wasn't easy to forgive. And by forgiving him, I'm not saying that what he did was okay, because it wasn't. But deciding to give up my feelings of hatred and resentment was a freeing experience, and it still is. I could move on with my life without the weight of anger and resentment that I had been carrying around for years. So I would like to challenge you to give up something meaningful for Lent, and surrender it to God. You won't believe how liberating it is!

Prayer: *Thank you, God, for forgiving me. Help us to be as forgiving of others. Amen.*

Thought for the day: Forgiveness set me free from emotional burdens.

Cindy Bear (Iowa, USA)

Why?

Read Job 11:7–16

'Why then did you bring me out of the womb?'
Job 10:18 (NIV)

As I was recovering from shoulder replacement surgery, all was going well – that is, until I broke out in shingles. Anyone who has ever experienced shingles knows that the pain and general misery are a nightmare. I confess I was angry at God.

I could relate in a very small way to what Job experienced. And, like Job, my prayers began with 'Why?' I was already extremely uncomfortable after surgery, and now this festering annoyance was getting worse each day! 'Why, God? What am I supposed to learn from this?'

I'm happy to say that the shingles wounds have healed, and my shoulder works better than ever. But I still don't understand what all that pain was supposed to teach me. Surely there is much in my life and in the world that just doesn't make sense. Sometimes we are not given the answers to our 'why' questions, but we can trust that God is with us. We can cry out to God with what we don't understand and know that God loves us still.

Prayer: *Loving God, help us to keep trusting you when our lives seem to be overly burdened. Strengthen our spirits, and walk with us through our struggles. Amen.*

Thought for the day: God is with me when things go right and when things go wrong.

Brenda Williams (Washington, USA)

Lost and found

Read 2 Corinthians 5:16–21

'This son of mine was dead and is alive again; he was lost and is found.' So they began to celebrate.
Luke 15:24 (NIV)

Graduating from university, studying abroad, earning a PhD, striving to be a good Christian – everything was going smoothly. However, at times I had experienced ups and downs. I worked days and nights without a break, repeatedly meeting with failures, and I became depressed.

Eventually I moved to a small town where I began to work for a kimchi manufacturing company. I felt like I was starting from nothing. Because I am clumsy and was inexperienced in manual labour, I often received criticism from my coworkers. All I could do was pray. I was weary from my repeated failures. But the Lord welcomed me with open arms even though I had lived like the prodigal son for decades (see Luke 15:11–32).

From that time, my life was changed. My thinking became peaceful and positive, I praised more and felt more gratitude, and when faced with a false accusation I was able to smile and carry on. These changes resulted from the love and acceptance of the Lord.

No matter what we do, the Lord embraces us. Jesus came to save sinners, and he looks for every lost sheep until he finds it. Those who wander away from the Lord can always come back. The Lord welcomes everyone with open arms.

Prayer: *Heavenly Father, thank you for waiting for us and forgiving our sins. May all people recognise your love and turn to you. Amen.*

Thought for the day: I will look for Jesus as eagerly as he looks for me.

Eui-mo Yang (Seoul, South Korea)

Words of love

Read Ephesians 4:25–32

Pleasant words are like a honeycomb, sweetness to the soul and health to the body.
Proverbs 16:24 (NRSV)

My high school English teacher assigned daily journal writing and collected the week's journal entries each Friday. One day, I wrote in my English journal about an embarrassing situation with another student. At the lockers between classes, I had dropped a textbook on the foot of a girl next to me. I apologised, but her angry reaction left me feeling ashamed and small, especially as she complained loudly to her friend. I wrote about my emotions, assuming the teacher didn't read our journals but simply checked that we had done the assignment. The following Monday, however, I found that my teacher had written a note in my journal. She pointed out the good qualities she noticed in me and encouraged me to view myself that way too. Although I felt a bit exposed, my teacher's caring, thoughtful response lifted my spirits.

Words carry weight. How we use them deeply impacts the people around us. That's why Paul instructs the Ephesians to throw off bitterness, rage and anger, replacing them with speech that benefits and builds up others. Even when sharing difficult truths, we can express ourselves with compassion. Each day brings opportunities to speak wholesome, helpful words to others.

Prayer: *Loving God, we pray that you will empower us to speak love and life to those around us. Give us compassionate and encouraging words. Amen.*

Thought for the day: With God's help, I will speak words that build others up.

Allison Wilson Lee (Florida, USA)

Giants in the land

Read Numbers 13:17–29

'The people who live there are powerful, and the cities are fortified and very large. We even saw descendants of Anak there.'
Numbers 13:28 (NIV)

When the spies Moses sent to the land of Canaan returned and gave their report, they had both good news and bad. They reported that the land truly flowed with milk and honey, and they brought fruit back with them. However, they also reported that the people living there were powerful, the cities were fortified and very large, and they saw descendants of Anak there. The descendants of Anak were giants, as described in Deuteronomy 9:2: 'These people are large and tall – they are the Anakim. You know and have heard what people say: "Who can stand up to the Anakim?"' (CEB).

Today we face our own giants. Although they look different from those described in Canaan, they instil fear in our lives. These fears can cause us to freeze up and stop trying to achieve our goals. But as giants appear in our lives, seemingly blocking the path towards our goals, we should not fear them. God is with us every step of the way and will fulfil every promise God has made to us.

Prayer: *Loving Father, thank you for keeping your promise to be with us today and every day. In Jesus' name. Amen.*

Thought for the day: No matter what giants I face, God is with me.

H. S. Radebe (South Africa)

Wrong number

Read Jeremiah 29:11–13

'You will call on me and come and pray to me, and I will listen to you.'
Jeremiah 29:12 (NIV)

In my childhood our telephone (a landline, of course) was a shared line, which meant that if I picked up the handset to make a phone call, it was possible that other people were already in the middle of a call and I could hear their conversation. I would then quickly put down the phone so their call remained private, and would have to wait until the line was clear.

While phone technology has advanced remarkably since those days, there are still limits to being able to connect with friends and loved ones. When we dial someone we can get a busy signal or a 'number unavailable' message, if the phone is in use or switched off. At other times, we can be in the middle of a phone conversation and the connection is cut off or we lose signal, and we have to redial to continue our talk. On a few occasions when we dial there is a 'wrong number' message, as the phone number is no longer in use or we have misdialled.

How wonderful to know that none of the above is true with God! Our heavenly Father is never unavailable. With him our conversations are private. He is never busy with another call or out of reach. We don't need to leave him a message and wait for him to call back. We are never cut off. And with God there is no 'wrong number'. He is always ready to listen, speak and help us. He will always answer in his perfect time.

Prayer: *Father, we thank you that we can depend on you to hear and answer our prayers, and that you are always there. Amen.*

Thought for the day: God is always ready to hear our prayers and calls to him.

Christine Hay (Scotland, United Kingdom)

Offering hope

Read Luke 7:11–17

Be joyful in hope, patient in affliction, faithful in prayer.
Romans 12:12 (NIV)

In Luke 7, Jesus saw the widow's grief as the body of her only son was being carried away. Jesus understood her deep sorrow and comforted her. But nobody was prepared for what Jesus did next. He did the impossible – he raised her son from the dead. Everyone was surprised and amazed. But Jesus did not perform this miracle just to impress the people. The mother felt hopeless, and Jesus gave her hope.

We all experience loss, be it the death of a loved one, a broken heart or an unfulfilled dream. Whatever we are going through, God is aware of our situation. Do not lose heart, for God is with us. In time, God will wipe away our tears, open other doors for us and bring new joy to our lives. Just as Jesus comforted the widow and brought her new joy and hope, he will comfort us and offer us hope too.

Prayer: *Loving God, thank you for knowing our joys and our sorrows. Comfort us and give us courage, helping us to stay strong and hope in you. Amen.*

Thought for the day: With God, I can always have hope.

Golda Dilema (Cavite, Philippines)

Fully charged

Read Isaiah 40:28–31

He gives strength to the weary and increases the power of the weak.
Isaiah 40:29 (NIV)

A friend's car battery was mysteriously losing its charge. The voltage would decrease while the car was parked overnight. After multiple trips to the mechanic, they found a small parasitic draw caused by a short in the wiring that was slowly draining the battery. They repaired the faulty wire, and the battery now stays fully charged.

Our inner spiritual energy supplied by the Holy Spirit likewise can be diminished by the parasitic draw of distractions and idols. Difficult news, social media, pride, grudges, greed, self-sufficiency, desire for recognition and success may all, like that faulty wire, steal our spiritual energy. This can lead us away from our relationship with God, from following Jesus and from serving others. But prayer, praise and worship, Bible study and fellowship with Christian friends restore our spiritual energy.

Prayer: *Lord God, thank you for the strength you give us. Help us resist the distractions and idols that sap our connection to you and to others. Amen.*

Thought for the day: What do I allow to steal my energy and separate me from God?

John R. Robinson (Georgia, USA)

Beautiful transformation

Read John 12:20–29

Your word is a lamp for my feet, a light on my path.
Psalm 119:105 (NIV)

A few months ago, I put a flowering potted plant in my garden. Unfortunately, scorching heat caused the plant to dry up. I thought it had died, but to my surprise a few days later I noticed new signs of life. Tiny green leaves began to appear, followed by little buds that blossomed into beautiful pink flowers. Even though the plant looked lifeless on the outside, there was still beautiful life within it.

While telling his disciples about his death, Jesus said, 'Unless a grain of wheat falls to the ground and dies, it remains only a single seed. But if it dies, it produces many seeds' (John 12:24). It is the same with us. When we let our sinful nature die, God's life-giving grace can begin redemptive work within us. As the light and love of God transform us, our lives become beautiful, fragrant and fruitful. Dark thoughts, despair and doubt can make us blind to God's love and grace, but scripture reminds us that God's love is always available. As we commune with God, we are strengthened and can bear much fruit. And when we 'die' to ourselves, we can see Christ glorified in and through us.

Prayer: *Loving God, thank you for your living word that transforms us into a new creation in Christ. Help us to surrender our lives so that we may bear much fruit for you. In Jesus' name. Amen.*

Thought for the day: I rejoice in God, who has given me new life through redemptive love.

Navamani Peter (Karnataka, India)

Comfort in hard times

Read 2 Corinthians 1:3–7

Just as we share abundantly in the sufferings of Christ, so also our comfort abounds through Christ.
2 Corinthians 1:5 (NIV)

In April 2000, I had just gotten home when the phone rang and I heard these words from a doctor in California: 'Your daughter has sustained a snow-boarding injury. We're sorry to tell you that she will never walk again.'

After absorbing the shock of this news, my husband, son and I boarded the next flight to see her. I had no way of knowing what lay ahead for her. But what I know in hindsight is this: God comforted us every step of the way during the following months and years. God provided encouragement from a woman in a wheelchair, lodging at the home of parents going through similar circumstances, and compassionate employers who continued to pay me as I stayed and learned, along with my daughter, about the different life she would now lead. I felt God's comfort in all of these details, even during my darkest moments.

Our daughter has gone through many surgeries over the years, and she has persevered and excelled. She has stayed in California and made a life on her own, leading a support group to help comfort others with spinal cord injuries. Praise God for the many forms of encouragement and comfort bestowed on us!

Prayer: *Gracious God, give hope to those who sustain life-changing injuries. Thank you that no matter what we experience, you are with us, providing comfort and hope. Amen.*

Thought for the day: Because God comforts me, I can extend comfort to others.

Patricia Vine (New Jersey, USA)

The light in the darkness

Read Philippians 4:4–7

Do not be anxious about anything, but in every situation, by prayer and petition, with thanksgiving, present your requests to God.
Philippians 4:6 (NIV)

When I was young, I slept with the light on in the bathroom down the hall because I was afraid of the dark. The light would shine into my bedroom, and I would hear the calming sound of the fan in the bathroom as I drifted off to sleep, feeling safe. Whenever the bathroom light wasn't on, I felt anxious, and it was much harder for me to fall asleep.

When Paul gave the command not to be anxious, he had greater reason to worry than does a kid who is afraid of the dark. He was in prison for proclaiming the gospel to the nations, and he was unsure of what his future held. In Paul's moment of uncertainty, he chose to focus his attention on the one who calls himself the light of the world.

When we aren't sure of where we are headed or how God will lead us, we can choose to trust in Christ and focus on the illuminating grace of his presence. Christ's light can guide us through the often tumultuous waves of life.

Prayer: *Dear God, help us to worry less and trust you to guide our steps. Amen.*

Thought for the day: When I feel worried, I will focus on Christ, the light of the world.

Cody Strawser (Ohio, USA)

It's the beginning

Read Isaiah 55:6–9

*'My thoughts are not your thoughts, neither are your ways my ways,'
declares the Lord. 'As the heavens are higher than the earth, so are my
ways higher than your ways and my thoughts than your thoughts.'*
Isaiah 55:8–9 (NIV)

'Why do you think the path ends here?' the tour guide asked while we
wandered the carefully curated grounds surrounding the castle. My
nine-year-old son volunteered, 'Maybe it isn't the end; maybe it's the
beginning.' We all smiled at this insightful perspective.

Several years earlier this same son had struggled to keep up with
handwriting in kindergarten, and that seemed like an ominous start to
his education. After much prayer we took him out of public school and
began teaching him at home. The end of my son's public education was
the beginning of many great years of our learning together, including
that castle tour with our home-school friends.

Life is full of roadblocks, and we can become discouraged thinking we
have reached the end. Isaiah reminds us that God's ways are different
from ours. God's perspective on our situation is much different than our
limited view. My son's observation on the path that day reminds me to
trust God's perspective no matter the circumstances and have hope that
what seems like an ending might also be a beginning.

Prayer: *Dear God, help us trust that you know our needs. Turn us from
despair, and help us to walk in faith. Amen.*

Thought for the day: I can trust God's perspective in difficult
circumstances.

Sherry Graf (Colorado, USA)

PRAYER FOCUS: TEACHERS AND HOME EDUCATORS

Receiving love

Read John 13:31–35

'A new command I give you: Love one another. As I have loved you, so you must love one another.'
John 13:34 (NIV)

I remember the first time anyone told me they loved me. When I was a child, my parents *showed* me love – they provided me with a home, fed and clothed me, bought me presents, looked after me when I was sick, and took me on trips when they could afford it. But they never actually said the words *I love you*. They were probably never told that they were loved as children either. As wonderful as my parents were, I doubted their love when I was younger, wondering if their kind actions towards me were motivated by a sense of duty.

The first person who told me they loved me was Ruthie, a three-year-old child from the church I was attending. I did not know how to respond. How could a three-year-old whom I barely knew tell me she loved me when my parents couldn't? Ruthie could tell me that she loved me because her parents had demonstrated and spoken of their love for her.

It is vitally important to know that we are loved – especially to know we are loved by God. Sometimes I sit quietly before the Lord, open my hands, and say, 'Jesus, I receive your love. Father, I receive your love.' And as I receive love from God, I can pass that love to others both through actions and words.

Prayer: *Thank you, Father, for sending your son to die for us, not out of duty but out of love. We open our hearts to receive your love today. Amen.*

Thought for the day: Today I will take time to sit in God's presence and receive God's love.

Mary Foulger (Ontario, Canada)

Why me?

Read James 1:2–12

We also glory in our sufferings, because we know that suffering produces perseverance; perseverance, character; and character, hope.
Romans 5:3–4 (NIV)

Prison is a breeding ground for human suffering. Having spent the better part of my adult life behind bars, I have witnessed much pain. Countless times I have cried out to God, 'Why me?' Today's scripture readings remind us that God can use our suffering to change lives. Central to that plan is the transformation of our spirits.

For many of us behind bars, we come to the point where the only place left to go is to our knees and cry out to God to forgive our transgressions and welcome us home like the prodigal son. I spend my days in here trying to be the man that God created me to be, trying to use my experience and years of suffering to help others. Today I take comfort in knowing that the Lord is using me as a vessel of compassion and love. Today I allow God to use my life as an example of true spiritual transformation. If we allow it, God will change us.

Prayer: *Merciful God, use us to demonstrate your ability to mend broken hearts and transform lives. Amen.*

Thought for the day: I will embrace my suffering knowing that God can use it for a greater good.

Christopher King (Virginia, USA)

God hears our cries

Read Romans 8:22–30

The Spirit helps us in our weakness. We do not know what we ought to pray for, but the Spirit himself intercedes for us through wordless groans.
Romans 8:26 (NIV)

My heart hammered in my chest and turmoil swirled inside me because my father was in hospital. However, attending a prayer gathering at my church with Christians from a variety of denominations and being surrounded by believers and God's loving presence was comforting. All of us were at different stages in our personal journeys with Jesus, but we all had hope and faith. I found the readings, thoughts and messages inspiring, even though there was a knot of worry inside me. When it was time to offer prayer requests, I desperately wanted to ask for a blessing for my dad; but if I were to speak, I knew my sadness would overcome me. I felt powerless and voiceless.

One of the parishioners who knew of my situation smiled at me, then stood up and prayed, 'We ask God to protect the sick and hospitalised who are suffering and need healing – and we ask God to help those who are caring for them.' Tears filled my eyes. Overcome with gratitude, I felt peace filling my soul. My loving heavenly Father had heard my cry and allowed someone else to give voice to my need.

Prayer: *Loving Father, thank you for listening to us and surrounding us with your love. Amen.*

Thought for the day: I take comfort knowing that God always listens to me.

Cindy Lee (England, United Kingdom)

Renewal

Read Hebrews 11:8–12

We walk by faith, not by sight.
2 Corinthians 5:7 (KJV)

In late December while I was walking our dog, I noticed the trees had lost their leaves and looked dead. I felt like those trees because I could see no evidence in my life of answered prayers. Later on, at the end of March, I observed the trees again. This time I noticed tiny buds poking out at the tips of the limbs. By the end of May the trees were covered with green leaves, ready to shade us from the summer sun.

When we don't see evidence of God at work in our lives, we may begin to doubt God and to think nothing will ever change. In Genesis, God tells Abraham at least four times that he would give him and Sarah a son. Years go by, but the child hasn't come. The last time God promises Abraham and Sarah a son, Sarah laughs because of the impossibility of the idea, especially at their ages. Despite their lack of faith, God reassures them: 'Is anything too hard for the Lord?' (Genesis 18:14). Sure enough, at God's appointed time Sarah gave birth to Isaac, and they got to witness God turn an impossibility into a reality.

Those barren trees reassured me that God can bring renewal to what may seem dead. If God takes care of the trees, surely God will take care of our concerns as well.

Prayer: *Heavenly Father, thank you for your promise that if we wait on you, we won't be disappointed. Amen.*

Thought for the day: My limited perception cannot limit God.

Brenda Brooks (Virginia, USA)

Building the kingdom

How do you feel about making New Year's resolutions? Do you eagerly make a list of resolutions for the year? Or do you reluctantly set some goals because it feels like you should? Sometimes people set resolutions to improve their life in some way. Sometimes our resolutions are shaped by external pressures. In any case, resolutions can be a helpful way to set goals and give us a sense of purpose.

In my experience, however, New Year's resolutions have often felt restrictive. I feel that unless I reach the goals I have set for myself, I am unworthy of relaxing or enjoying the present. I think, *When I'm in better shape, then I'll be able to do this or that. When I've read more books… When I've broken this bad habit…* And the list goes on.

It's not just New Year's resolutions that take on this pattern. We might find ourselves thinking throughout the year that our lives will be better when we've made more space for rest, when we have a different job, when our child gets older or when a parent is no longer in the hospital. So often, we set goals or imagine futures where we will have time, capacity and energy to do the things that feel important but impossible in the present moment. It's a cycle that keeps us comparing the present to what used to be and waiting for perfect scenarios or ideal conditions. And, ironically, most of the time this cycle keeps us stuck where we are – dissatisfied and longing for something different.

I think Jesus understood this tendency to want everything to be in order before moving on to the next task. When he tells the people, 'Let the dead bury their own dead' (Luke 9:60, NRSV) and 'No one who puts a hand to the plough and looks back is fit for the kingdom of God' (v. 62), I think he is speaking to this common human plight. Though these statements sound harsh to us who want everything to be settled before we take up the next task, I think perhaps Jesus is saying, 'You are enough *now*. You don't need to fix, improve or finish anything to be my disciple. Let go of what feels urgent and what holds you back. Follow me and set a new priority – building the kingdom of God with what *is* right here and now.'

Certainly, to build a kingdom, we need a vision, priorities and resources, but none of those requires us to meet any particular standard of living or accomplishment before we can participate. God calls us to love our neighbours and ourselves just as we are – no improvements required. Jesus already set the vision and priorities for what this new kingdom will look like: 'Blessed are you who are poor, for yours is the kingdom of God' (Luke 6:20). Luke goes on to say, 'People will come from east and west, from north and south, and take their places… in the kingdom of God' (Luke 13:29). Indeed, following Jesus means living in such a way that everyone around us can experience God's kingdom drawing near. When we feed those who are hungry, heal those who are sick, provide shelter to those who need it, offer hospitality to those who are new to our communities, and choose to see all people as God's children, we are building the kingdom of God.

Let the dead bury their own dead. I think the invitation here is for us to let go of all that holds us back, and to let go of the image of future perfection that keeps us from being fully present here and now. How might we enter this new year not with resolutions that tie us to the past but by following Christ into the future towards God's kingdom?

QUESTIONS FOR REFLECTION

1 In this new year, what will you leave behind? What expectations for yourself and others will you release?

2 How will you focus on building the kingdom of God this year?

Lindsay Gray, editorial director, The Upper Room

A pattern of prayer

Read Psalm 119:1–8

Blessed are those… who walk according to the law of the Lord.
Psalm 119:1 (NIV)

My husband, Gary, and I enjoy morning walks. We enjoy the fresh air, vent about problems and make plans for the future. When I walk daily, I am eager to get out and move – and I have more energy. But on days when the weather is bad, I tend to hunker down inside, letting Gary walk alone. The longer I avoid walking, the less enthusiasm I have for it.

My prayer life follows a similar pattern. When I simply offer a few quick prayers during the day, my prayers tend to skitter along the surface like a flat pebble across a lake. However, when I spend the time in longer, deeper prayer, I become more eager to reach out to God again. Prayer then becomes a regular and meaningful part of my day.

We all have places in our lives where we could improve spiritually. I find it helpful to set a specific goal – for example, reading a chapter of the Bible each day or praying for a set amount of time every morning – then finding an accountability partner to hold me to it until the habit becomes a natural part of life. Morning walks can improve our health, but walking with God enriches the soul.

Prayer: *Faithful God, thank you for all the ways we can draw closer to you. Help us to walk daily in the presence of your Holy Spirit. Amen.*

Thought for the day: I will make it a habit to walk daily with God.

Susan Thogerson Maas (Oregon, USA)

Draw near to God

Read Romans 8:32–39

Let us then approach God's throne of grace with confidence, so that we may receive mercy and find grace to help us in our time of need.
Hebrews 4:16 (NIV)

I normally wear cologne, but I have had to stop. My daughter suffers from asthma, and we work in the same office. Her doctor advised her to avoid all perfumes and fragrances to minimise her allergies. She and I share a close bond, and her natural tendency is to give hugs often. So I have stopped using cologne.

Ephesians 5:2 says, 'Christ loved us and gave himself up for us as a fragrant offering and sacrifice to God.' As I made a small sacrifice for my daughter, I began to reflect on Christ's sacrifice for us. Christ offered himself up on the cross to restore the lost bond between us and God. He relinquished all his glory and majesty so that we all could draw close to God. In accepting and doing God's will, Christ received God's blessing and recognition. Now he sits at the right hand of God as the connection that allows humankind to draw near to God.

Prayer: *Jesus, our Lord and Redeemer, we give you thanks for your sacrifice that made it possible for us to draw near to God. Your presence is the balm that adds fragrance to our lives. Amen.*

Thought for the day: Because of Christ, I can draw near to God.

Juan Julio Báez (Dominican Republic)

God of light

Read Isaiah 58:6–12

Let the righteous be joyful; let them exult before God; let them be jubilant with joy.
Psalm 68:3 (NRSV)

I stared at the calendar, and my heart sank. Years before, on the first day of spring, my son had died unexpectedly. This year the anniversary of his death fell on a Sunday, and although I wanted to stay home, God urged me to go to church. During the children's time in the worship service, the leader used a flashlight to teach the children about sharing Jesus' light with others. Memories of my son in Sunday school came flooding back.

As the children left the sanctuary, one little boy skipped towards the door shouting, 'This will be amazing!' After a few giggles, the congregation turned their attention back to the pastor, but I kept thinking about the boy. Through the excitement in his voice and spring in his step, the light of Jesus spread into my heart.

It's sometimes easy for despair to douse the light of Jesus. I had arrived at church feeling low. However, God helped me realise that sharing the light of Christ with others is a way of honouring my son. On my walk that afternoon, birds sang and flowers bloomed. I collected empty cans in the road to recycle as my son would have done. Shining through dense, grey clouds were streams of sunlight. The little boy was right; this day was amazing!

Prayer: *God of light, we thank you. Continue to illuminate our hearts and brighten our spirits. Help us to better serve you. In your Son Jesus' name we pray. Amen.*

Thought for the day: No matter my grief, the light of Jesus will always surround me.

Kelly Desclos-Estes (Virginia, USA)

A family feud

Read Mark 11:25–26

Love your enemies, bless them that curse you, do good to them that hate you, and pray for them which despitefully use you, and persecute you.

Matthew 5:44 (KJV)

I inherited a family feud that had been going on for over 50 years. It was a battle over land, passed down from generation to generation. It's called 'heir property', and it can be messy when everyone wants the same lot. During court preparations, I received a court document that upset me to the point of anger.

I wanted to retaliate with words of my own. My mind was racing with all I wanted to say. Anger is not a fruit of the Spirit, and I needed a listening ear. I called a friend and explained the situation. Honestly, I wanted to hear my friend say, 'She did what?' thus adding fuel to my fire. But instead, my spiritual sister asked, 'Have you prayed for her? What's her name?' And so we prayed. What a revelation! Prayer changed my entire focus, and I began to call out my cousin's name in my daily prayers.

As it turned out, court was avoided, and God brought a 50-year feud to an end with a compromise. I gained more than land that day; I gained a new perspective, which led me to apologise. Prayers for the people in our conflicts take our mind off the anger and hurt and put our focus on a new life in Christ for all involved.

Prayer: *Dear Lord, thank you for forgiving us. Help us to forgive others as you have forgiven us. Amen.*

Thought for the day: Praying for others helps me focus on what matters most.

Rhonda Thomas (Maryland, USA)

My rock and my fortress

Read Psalm 18:1–15

The Lord is my rock, my fortress and my deliverer.
Psalm 18:2 (NIV)

After graduation, I was looking forward to my dream job of joining the Defence Force to serve my nation. Unfortunately, I did not get a good enough score to be eligible. So I pursued my master's degree and became eligible to take the entrance exam – it felt like my last chance to make or break my dream career.

My family and I prayed for my interview and other tests, asking that I would be selected for a job. With God's grace, I was selected.

During training, I started to lose hope that I would make it through. But God comforted me with confidence and strength to overcome my situation. Against the odds, I made it through, bringing joy to me, my family and my community.

God never leaves us in our struggles. When we depend on God, our rock and strong fortress, we find the hope and perseverance to patiently wait on God's deliverance.

Prayer: *Faithful God, thank you for the ways you comfort and guide us through our struggles. Give us hope and patience as we trust in your will for our lives. Amen.*

Thought for the day: When I hold fast to God, I will find hope and strength.

V. Ronald Levis (Uttar Pradesh, India)

Let God in

Read Matthew 4:1–11

Then Jesus was led by the Spirit into the wilderness to be tempted by the devil.

Matthew 4:1 (NIV)

What are you giving up for Lent? I know I am supposed to give up something in order to reflect on Jesus' 40 days in the desert and to prepare for the commemoration of Jesus' death and resurrection. My immediate answer for way too many years has been 'chocolate' and 'playing Pickleball.' But if I knew I was going to die in 40 days, giving up food and fun would not make the list at all! So, what would I give up?

I'd give up wasting time. I would focus on all the people I haven't seen or talked to enough and tell them how much they mean to me.

I'd give up trying to tell my grandkids what to do! Instead, I would write down my life's story – hopefully to leave answers to questions they will surely have after I am gone.

I'd give up harboured anger, resentment and frustration over my failures, the relationships that turned out badly, and the opportunities I ignored.

I'd give it all up to let God in – not just for Lent or 40 days, but from this day forward. Let us renew our commitment to follow Jesus' example of obedience as we seek fullness of life in God.

Prayer: *Dear God, help us to appreciate the sacrifice Jesus made for us. And give us the courage to follow his leading towards wholeness of life. Amen.*

Thought for the day: I will practise the disciplines of Lent every day.

Judy Hoyt Pettigrew (Florida, USA)

Childlike faith

Read 1 Samuel 17:32–37, 45–50
'Truly I tell you, anyone who will not receive the kingdom of God like a little child will never enter it.'
Mark 10:15 (NIV)

Eli was four years old and learning to swim. He could cross the shallow end of the pool with ease, but he had been afraid of swimming across the deep end. Then in one swim lesson, Eli did it.

As we were walking up to the house, I encouraged him about his monumental accomplishment. I asked him, 'How did you do it?' Without hesitation, Eli said, 'God helped me.' I thought, *If only my first thought would be, 'God helped me', when I face huge challenges in my life! Where would I be in my walk with God?*

Jesus loved children for their simple faith. They were willing to climb up into his arms and rest, knowing that Jesus loved and protected them. God's power is made perfect in childlike faith. David demonstrated childlike faith when he used a stone from the stream to slay Goliath (see 1 Samuel 17). The stones weren't magical, but David's faith in God overpowered the giant.

The next time we face overwhelming fear, I pray we have the childlike faith to cross the deep end and entrust ourselves to God. God will help us!

Prayer: *Dear God, the next time we face overwhelming fear help us to trust you with childlike faith. Amen.*

Thought for the day: God is my helper.

David E. Hedrick (Georgia, USA)

God's unfailing love

Read Ephesians 3:14–19

In him and through faith in him we may approach God with freedom and confidence.

Ephesians 3:12 (NIV)

I awoke with questions in my mind: *What if my mum had not gotten sick? What is life like for her now – for my father and our whole family? What if we didn't have to deal with this illness in the middle of a pandemic?*

My mum's first online consultation with the gastroenterologist was more than a year ago. What we thought to be a simple diagnosis of an upset stomach ended with a series of tests and medical procedures, including two biopsies. The initial biopsy suggested a benign condition. But my mum's stomach pain persisted, and she needed another series of tests and hospitalisations. Finally she was diagnosed with pancreatic cancer.

When my 'what if' questions became long and tiring, I began to pray. I did not want to dwell on those questions which were not only unanswerable but unhealthy and unhelpful. As I began crying out to the Lord for help, suddenly I felt at peace. My heart felt the love of God and the love of my family. Daily video calls with my mum and other family members became an expression of love and devotion for one another, and I enjoyed seeing their happy faces.

God hears our cries for help and comforts us. When we pray, God will draw us closer, giving us an awareness of God's unfailing love and living hope.

Prayer: *Heavenly Father, thank you for your unfailing love. Help us remember to come to you for guidance when troubles overwhelm us. Amen.*

Thought for the day: God hears and answers my cries for help.

Lei Cao Garcia-Bote (Kuala Lumpur, Malaysia)

Our true worth

Read 1 Samuel 16:6–12

The Lord said to Samuel… 'God doesn't look at things like humans do. Humans see only what is visible to the eyes, but the Lord sees into the heart.'
1 Samuel 16:7 (CEB)

I was listening to a Catholic deacon talking on the radio. Before going into ministry, he had been an auctioneer at Sotheby's in London, and he was asked what surprising valuations still stuck in his mind. He recounted how a little brown ball that was brought in turned out to be a Victorian-era golf ball worth over £12,000. He commented, 'It is often things that don't look as though they would have any value that turn out to be very valuable.' That inauspicious golf ball could so easily have been discarded!

Sometimes we can be the same way with people, even in our churches – judging their worth by their outward appearance. They might not be particularly attractive, talented, outgoing or confident. They may be on the margins of society. They may not show gifts that are obvious to others.

When God sent Samuel to anoint one of Jesse's sons as the new king of Israel, Samuel started judging Jesse's sons by how they looked – how tall or how handsome they were. But God directed Samuel to David, the youngest brother. The Lord told Samuel that he judges people not by how they look, but by what is in their hearts.

The good news of Jesus is that we all have inherent value to God. We all have a unique beauty and worth to him who is more concerned with what is in our hearts than our appearances.

Prayer: *Lord, may we see beyond the outward appearances of those we meet today and value them as you do.*

Thought for the day: I am of immeasurable worth to God.

Faith Ford (England, United Kingdom)

A handmade gift

Read Psalm 118:15–24

This is the day which the Lord hath made; we will rejoice and be glad in it.
Psalm 118:24 (KJV)

Have you ever been given something made by hand? Perhaps someone gifted you a meal from their kitchen, a flower arrangement from their garden or a one-of-a-kind craft. Similarly, each day is a gift from our creator that we can receive with gladness.

Sometimes the person receiving the gift may not always understand the time and effort required to make a handmade gift. And we may not feel like rejoicing each and every day when we are facing trials or feeling ill. But before my feet hit the floor in the morning, I practise reciting this verse: 'This is the day the Lord has made, and I will rejoice and be glad in it!'

Each morning I choose to be thankful and pray that my presence will be a reflection of the light of our creator, the maker of heaven and earth. Let us give thanks for God's gift of today and enter each day with a spirit of rejoicing.

Prayer: *Creator of heaven and earth, help us to know you and to recognise the works of your hands. We will rejoice and be glad, giving thanks for the gift of each day. Amen.*

Thought for the day: I will give thanks to God for the gift of each day.

Robin Bullock (Florida, USA)

Strength in the storm

Read Matthew 7:24–29

'Everybody who hears these words of mine and puts them into practice is like a wise builder who built a house on bedrock.'
Matthew 7:24 (CEB)

Where I live, we have had a very wet summer with some violent thunderstorms. The rain has been relentless, trees have been uprooted and rivers are swollen and overflowing. During one storm, water gushed under the back door of our home. This made me think of Jesus' story about the two men who each built a house: one on the sand and one on the rock.

No doubt the sky was clear and bright when the first man built his house on the sand. He wasn't contemplating any storms. The other man considered that storms must inevitably come to all of us, so he built his house on the rock. When the first storm came, the house on the sand collapsed, while the one on the rock withstood the weather.

If we keep spiritually strong by reading the Bible, praying, engaging in spiritual practices and worshipping with fellow believers in Christ, we can recover from adverse circumstances more easily. When our lives are grounded and firmly set on the Rock and his teachings, we can weather the storms that come our way.

Prayer: *Dear Lord, help us to faithfully build our lives on you and what you are teaching us. Help us to be bold in our witness and to stand strong with you. Amen.*

Thought for the day: When the storms of life are raging, Jesus stands with me.

Valerie Clark (KwaZulu-Natal, South Africa)

God sees us

Read Mark 5:35–43

He gave them strict orders that no one should know what had happened. Then he told them to give her something to eat.
Mark 5:43 (CEB)

In Mark 5, Jesus exorcised a demon, healed a woman of her haemorrhage and raised a little girl from the dead. I would have guessed that after all that, Jesus would have rubbed his hands together and called it a day. Or maybe he would have sat back among a crowd to recount all that he had done. That is what I would have done. But that was not Jesus' way.

Jesus was more concerned about the risen girl's needs. She was not a project to him; she was not a means to make himself look better. Jesus saw the young girl as a person with needs and fears. While everyone else was ecstatic and shocked, Jesus saw that the girl was hungry and told her mother and father to give her some food.

In God's eyes we are not means to an end. We are not just one of many pieces in the puzzle. To God, each one of us is a person with our own needs and fears. God is interested in even the tiniest details of our lives. In every moment, remember that there is nothing too trivial to bring to God.

Prayer: *Dear God, may we always remember that nothing is too trivial to bring to you. As your people we thank you for always caring about us. Amen.*

Thought for the day: God sees me and my needs and will care for me.

Bob LaForge (New Jersey, USA)

In God's time

Read Isaiah 43:14–21

'Forget the former things; do not dwell on the past. See, I am doing a new thing! Now it springs up; do you not perceive it? I am making a way in the wilderness and streams in the wasteland.'
Isaiah 43:18–19 (NIV)

One spring during my morning walks, I noticed my neighbour building a brick walkway from his porch to the street. Gradually over several weeks, I watched as he prepared the ground, poured gravel and laid bricks. Then for some reason I could not perceive, I saw that he had ripped up half the path and piled the bricks in his yard. Eventually, the path was completed, and the mess was cleaned up. If I had not been paying attention, the finished path might have seemed to appear overnight. But I had witnessed the process: the planning, measuring, waiting, ripping up and restarting.

The construction of my neighbour's walkway illustrates that sometimes things don't happen overnight – even when God is doing something new in our lives and inviting us to grow from it. Isaiah 43:18–19 reminds me to keep my eyes open for how God is at work in my life.

Growth is a process – one step at a time. We can trust that God is always doing something new. As we become more aware of God's presence, we can watch for the new things God is doing, give thanks and proclaim God's great work.

Prayer: *Dear God, we praise your name and proclaim the new and wondrous works you do in our lives. Amen.*

Thought for the day: God is always doing something new in my life.

Tracie Heskett (Washington, USA)

Our true refuge

Read Psalm 27

The Lord of hosts is with us; the God of Jacob is our refuge.
Psalm 46:7 (NRSV)

One cloudy morning, my husband and I set out for our usual walk in our neighbourhood. When we were far from home, it suddenly started to rain and a strong wind picked up. We ran to the covered steps of a church, where we took shelter until the storm passed.

The church is a place of prayer, a house of worship. But as I sat on the steps that day, I realised that many times in our Christian walk we don't have access to the physical shelter of a church. Regardless, the house of God shall remain open because we have the presence of the Holy Spirit within our souls. All we truly need is the Lord! God welcomes us and protects us.

Life confronts us all with struggles – the separation of loved ones, chronic illness, unemployment, disappointment with friends or family. But even in our most difficult times, the unconditional and welcoming love of God through Jesus Christ holds us, strengthens us and keeps us going.

Prayer: *Loving God, we thank you that your shelter is available to us wherever we are. Remind us to seek refuge in you. Amen.*

Thought for the day: No matter my situation, I can find shelter in God.

Lucy Ferraz de Almeida Pezzolo (São Paulo, Brazil)

Uncertain times

Read Hebrews 11:1–16

Faith is confidence in what we hope for and assurance about what we do not see.

Hebrews 11:1 (NIV)

My wife and I sat in a neurologist's office to discuss the results of her MRI and the clinical insights of her documented falls, memory lapses, tremors and other symptoms. My wife was diagnosed with a rare disorder of the brain known as progressive supranuclear palsy. The condition has no definitive diagnostic test, no known cause and no cure.

In today's scripture reading, we find that even the greatest of Bible characters were like us. They faced uncertain times, they didn't always receive all they hoped for, things didn't always go their way. However, like all of us, by faith they possessed a 'longing for a better country – a heavenly one' (v. 16). And God prepares the heavenly place which will ultimately satisfy all our longings!

Peace and joy are not dependent on our circumstances, but on the promises of God. We know beyond this earthly journey awaits an indescribable, wonderful, eternal life. Faith is indeed having 'confidence in what we hope for and assurance about what we do not see'.

Prayer: *Dear Lord, even during times when we may not feel your presence, thank you for always being with us. Your love endures forever. Amen.*

Thought for the day: Times of uncertainty help me appreciate the certainty of God's promises.

Larry Scanlan (Maryland, USA)

God's shadow

Read Psalm 91

Whoever dwells in the shelter of the Most High will rest in the shadow of the Almighty.
Psalm 91:1 (NIV)

In Scotland, we don't have a lot of warm sunshine. I remember as a teenager sitting outdoors sunbathing, trying to get a tan. I'd sigh with disappointment when a cloud obscured the sun temporarily, covering me in a cool shadow.

My feelings towards shadows changed dramatically when I landed in Madras, India, in May 1975 to serve on the staff of a teacher-training college. I stepped off the plane into what felt like a hot oven – 43 degrees Celcius. Overhead was a cloudless blue sky. In what can be an oppressively hot and humid climate, people long for a shadow under which to shelter. The students used to sit in groups under the spreading foliage of trees to study together.

Likewise, in the warm, sunny land of Israel, where David composed his psalms, a shadow would be thought of as a gift, a comfort, a protection – something to be valued. How much more valuable, then, is 'the shadow of the Almighty'! In God's shadow, we are surely safe and secure.

Prayer: *Dear God, thank you for the change in perspective new experiences can bring. Inspire us today to rest in your wonderful shadow. Amen.*

Thought for the day: I am safe and secure in the Lord.

Lynda Samuel (Scotland, United Kingdom)

The power of words

Read Luke 6:27–36

Hatred stirs up strife, but love covers all offences.
Proverbs 10:12 (NRSV)

I only had one brother. He was six years older than me, and joined the navy when I was 13. As we got older, we bonded over our common interest in amateur radio.

On one of our family's visits to his house, he and I retreated to his radio room and started talking. After a while he said, 'You sure hate a lot of things.' His words stopped me cold; he was right. I hated how that politician acted. I hated that product. I hated my income taxes. I realised that even though I claimed to be a Christian, I was living a life full of small hatreds. I would like to say I have completely overcome that mindset; but while I never say I 'hate' things anymore, I can still be critical of those who disagree with me.

Words of hatred and superiority can slip into our conversation, demeaning not only the subject of our talk but God's word as well. 'A word fitly spoken is like apples of gold in a setting of silver' (Proverbs 25:11). All people were made in God's image and deserve to be treated fairly and honourably. I have found if we look deep inside others, we may find people very much like ourselves.

Prayer: *O Lord, help us to avoid the trap of careless and negative words. Even when our words are critical, may we speak always with compassion. In Jesus' name. Amen.*

Thought for the day: Hateful words are easily spoken, but God calls me to caring speech.

Ken Claar (Idaho, USA)

Our rock

Read Psalm 31:1–5

Since you are my rock and my fortress, for the sake of your name lead and guide me.
Psalm 31:3 (NIV)

I live on an island with many beautiful beaches. When I feel the gentle rush of the waves, I reflect on the grandeur of God's divine creation. Starfish and snails of all shapes and colours reveal God's greatness and how detail-oriented the creator is.

One day, filled with admiration as I walked on the edge of the beach, I found a rock. Many types of algae floated about, entangled with each other. But one type of small, living algae was attached to the rock. This find allowed me to reflect on how God also gives us abundant life in troubled times.

Just as the algae found the rock, its source of life, in spite of the turbulent waters, so we can find Christ. He is our rock, our strength and protection, who gives us abundant life amid the challenges our lives can bring.

Prayer: *Creator God, help us always to remember that you are our rock and fortress. We pray as Jesus taught us: 'Our Father which art in heaven, Hallowed be thy name. Thy kingdom come, Thy will be done in earth, as it is in heaven. Give us this day our daily bread. And forgive us our debts, as we forgive our debtors. And lead us not into temptation, but deliver us from evil: For thine is the kingdom, and the power, and the glory, for ever. Amen' (Matthew 6:9–13, KJV).*

Thought for the day: Christ is my rock and my fortress.

Lydia E. Cruz Algarín (Puerto Rico)

Precious opportunity

Read John 15:5–8

Very early in the morning, while it was still dark, Jesus got up, left the house and went off to a solitary place, where he prayed.
Mark 1:35 (NIV)

Recently my husband and I took a trip across the country by train and car to visit my sister at her new home. I had never before seen the parts of the country we travelled through, and the journey was a thrill to me. However, the change of routine completely disrupted my habit of starting each day with prayer and quiet meditation.

Back home in my comfy chair with the cat curled up by my side, I took up my daily practice again. I reflected that I had seen so many amazing sights yet had not taken time to marvel at the creator. I had enjoyed the hospitality of my sister and brother-in-law but had not expressed gratitude to God for the good health and the means that allowed me to travel.

The Bible records that Jesus often went off to a solitary place to pray. Our Lord and Saviour took time alone to speak with God. That loving relationship is open to me as well. I realised that my devotional time is not a routine that I must leave behind when I go on holiday. It's a precious opportunity to thank God for all my blessings, speak whatever burden is on my heart, and ask for guidance every day.

Prayer: *Ever-present God, thank you for the opportunity to be in your presence day by day. May we never forget to thank you. Amen.*

Thought for the day: No matter where I am, I can spend time with God each day.

Betsy Mitchell (New York, USA)

Guiding light

Read Matthew 5:13–16

'You are the light of the world. A city built on a hill cannot be hid.'
Matthew 5:14 (NRSV)

Travelling on a ship at night gave me a new appreciation for the power of light. The lights on the ship shone brightly, but the open sea was dark and scary. I could not see anything, but I imagined the vast body of water. It made me feel helpless.

But then in the early morning, as we neared the port, we could see the light from a lighthouse on a hill. Through the darkness, the light in the distance guided our ship towards the port. That beacon made my heart leap with joy and gave me a sense of comfort.

Like a lighthouse in the dark, Christians can show God's light to weary souls through our actions. Kindness allows people to experience the goodness of the love and life of our Saviour Jesus Christ. When people are lost in the open sea of life's struggles, the light of Christ shines bright. Many are weary, longing for rest and comfort. We can be a beacon for them, guiding them to find comfort in God.

Prayer: *Dear Jesus, help us to keep our lights shining amid the challenges we face so that we may help others find their way. Amen.*

Thought for the day: When I show kindness and love to others, I bring light to their lives.

Paul Kurpengmund Anda (East Sepik, Papua New Guinea)

The power of prayer

Read Psalm 66:16–20

Pray continually.
1 Thessalonians 5:17 (NIV)

There was a period of three years in my life when I faced the loss of my mother-in-law to cancer, the death of a dear aunt, and the reality that I would never give birth to a child. One Sunday morning while listening to prayer requests in church, I heard someone say, 'Our prayers are working.' It angered me to hear those words. My prayers had not been answered. Were my prayers even heard? Why would the prayers of other believers be answered but not mine?

It took some time, but I came to realise that though my prayers did not reverse the outcomes of those situations in my life, my prayers did change me. Prayer helped me deal with the passing of loved ones and encouraged me to better love those who are here with me. Prayer gave me the ability to open my heart and mind to the possibility of adoption; my husband and I now share our life and home with a beautiful son. God did hear my prayers.

The answers to our prayers may not be what we have hoped, but there will be answers. Do not give up on prayer; it is working.

Prayer: *Dear God, help us to believe that you hear us when we pray and to trust that you will answer. Amen.*

Thought for the day: Prayer draws me closer to God.

Sheryl Black Chai (Tennessee, USA)

Opportunities to serve

Read Ecclesiastes 9:7–12

We're praying this so that you can live lives that are worthy of the Lord and pleasing to him in every way: by producing fruit in every good work and growing in the knowledge of God.
Colossians 1:10 (CEB)

After enjoying the first few months of retirement, I found that days of fun and relaxation do not always bring the peace and contentment I thought they would. Some days I have too much free time on my hands. It's frustrating for me not having a schedule.

As I have taken this to the Lord in prayer, asking for guidance about how to spend my time, I have received a surprising answer. I have learned that even those unscheduled hours have God's purpose stamped on them. Sometimes the purpose may be to teach me patience or to have a positive attitude no matter what is happening – or not happening – that day. The Bible says we are to 'give thanks in all circumstances; for this is God's will for you in Christ Jesus' (1 Thessalonians 5:18, NIV).

As I have accepted unplanned times of rest and relaxation, God has given me peace. I'm not rushing through my day, and I have the glorious privilege of spending more time studying scripture and in prayer. Having a more leisurely pace to my days has opened up new opportunities to serve: taking ice cream to a friend recovering from surgery, helping friends clean and pack for a move or sitting with a cancer patient during chemo treatments. I have found God's peace in the unplanned moments.

Prayer: *Almighty Father, our time is in your hands. Help us to serve you each and every day. In Jesus' name we pray. Amen.*

Thought for the day: Unscheduled hours open up opportunities to serve God.

Lucinda J. Rollings (Indiana, USA)

PRAYER FOCUS: SOMEONE WHO HAS RECENTLY RETIRED

Our source of power

Read Psalm 139:1–12

'The people living in darkness have seen a great light; on those living in the land of the shadow of death a light has dawned.'
Matthew 4:16 (NIV)

It is six o'clock on a cold winter morning, and I am in darkness. The power will be off for more than two hours, as our national power grid is no longer sufficient to supply the needs of our population. To eke out and share the available power, we have rotational power outages known as 'rolling blackouts' or 'load-shedding'.

But the world outside is not completely dark. In the street, the bright lights of cars move boldly through the darkness. These vehicles carry within themselves a power source that constantly regenerates.

I liken these vehicles to faithful Christians, who relentlessly move forward in an often dark world. When the power of the world is no longer sufficient to sustain us, we have a continuous and never-failing power source available to us – the light of Christ. We carry Christ's love within ourselves and regenerate it through studying scripture, worshipping and loving others even as we move forward in the darkness.

Prayer: *Source of light, we praise you and thank you for all the beacons that you place along our path to direct us and lead us to your never-failing light and love. Amen.*

Thought for the day: Because of my faith, I always have light in the darkness.

Keith Honeyman (Western Cape, South Africa)

Palm Sunday

Read John 12:12–19

They took branches of palm trees and went out to meet him, shouting, 'Hosanna! Blessed is the one who comes in the name of the Lord – the King of Israel!'
John 12:13 (NRSV)

Soon after Jesus resurrected Lazarus from the dead, a crowd of excited people followed him to Jerusalem. As Jesus rode in on a donkey, I wonder if Lazarus walked along with the crowd, waving palm branches to signify that Jesus was a great deliverer. I imagine that first Palm Sunday would have been personal for Lazarus as he walked with and worshipped his friend and hero who had just given him new life.

Easter is my favourite holiday because it reminds me of how I once went from death to life. When I first prayed asking Jesus to forgive my sins and come into my life, I had a momentary sensation of warm oil pouring over my head. I felt inner peace, as if I had just walked out of a tomb, and I began to hunger for more, reading scripture as if it were God's personal letter to me.

We all can welcome Jesus' entry into our lives every day. He is our Lord and Saviour, our personal deliverer, who conquered death and called each of us out of a tomb. We can trust in him each day to deliver us, bring peace to our minds and lead us to an abundant life.

Prayer: *Dear Jesus, we welcome you into our lives today. Thank you for giving us victory over sin and death. Amen.*

Thought for the day: Every day, Jesus enters my life in a new way.

Maria Barroso (Illinois, USA)

Using our gifts

Read Acts 9:36–42

In Joppa there was a disciple whose name was Tabitha, which in Greek is Dorcas. She was devoted to good works and acts of charity.
Acts 9:36 (NRSV)

When my mother passed away, I inherited her sewing basket, filled to the brim with thread, needles and every conceivable sewing accessory. I was pleased to have this keepsake, but I cannot sew a stitch! I have always admired individuals who possess sewing skills, those like Dorcas, whose story of generosity is recorded in Acts.

Dorcas was not only talented at sewing, but she unselfishly shared the garments she made with friends. In fact, Dorcas was so admired for her generosity that the apostle Peter immediately left the nearby city where he was ministering to come to Dorcas' house when he heard that she had died. There several widows proudly showed Peter the clothing Dorcas had sewn for them. When Peter brought Dorcas back to life, Acts records that many people came to believe in the Lord.

I cannot help but believe that many came to know Jesus as Saviour through the gift of Dorcas' sewing. While I am not a seamstress, I have other gifts I can use to share the love of Christ. Each of us has our own gifts we can use to help others know our Lord.

Prayer: *Dear Lord, help us to use our gifts to do good and to help those in need. Amen.*

Thought for the day: God shows me how to use my gifts for good.

Rita Hays (Tennessee, USA)

God goes with you

Read Deuteronomy 31:1–8

'Be strong and bold; have no fear or dread of them, because it is the Lord your God who goes with you; he will not fail you or forsake you.'
Deuteronomy 31:6 (NRSV)

'Where did all the days go?' I wondered aloud as I stared at my planner. As a soon-to-be mum with only a month left before my expected due date, I was growing more anxious each day. I had so many things I had not yet prepared. Our finances were tight, which made me all the more intimidated about our new responsibilities and our future hospital bill. On top of that, I had never taken care of a baby before. An incredible sense of insecurity and helplessness crept into my heart. I felt overwhelmed with feelings of inadequacy.

My husband heard my question and came to me. He embraced me and patted my back to comfort me. He read something from my planner that I had written a few weeks back: 'Be strong and bold; have no fear or dread of them, because it is the Lord your God who goes with you; he will not fail you or forsake you.'

I have known this verse for so long that at times I have felt extremely casual towards it. However, in that moment of great fear, it consoled me. It was as if my heavenly Father came to hold me and remind me in that exact moment: 'I go with you.' I did not need to live in dread of my insecurities.

Prayer: *Loving Father, thank you that you will never leave us or forsake us. Help us to live in this truth daily. In Jesus' name. Amen.*

Thought for the day: I do not need to dread the future, for God is with me.

Quennie Joyce Ibarra (Cagayan, Philippines)

A servant of God

Read James 2:14–26

We are what he has made us, created in Christ Jesus for good works, which God prepared beforehand so that we may walk in them.
Ephesians 2:10 (NRSV)

I spent many years as a volunteer for a local food programme. Each day, we delivered hot meals to folks who were unable to leave home to get their own food. We got to know the people we delivered to quite well, and we always arranged our schedule so that we could spend a few minutes visiting with each person.

One day, a woman to whom I was delivering food told me, 'You are truly a servant of God.' I was stunned. I had considered myself a volunteer and nothing more. But the more I thought about it, the more I realised that I was doing what the Lord asked his followers to do – spending time serving others.

There are many ways to serve God. We help make our world a better place when we live God's words and do God's work. Not only do we transform the lives of others, but we transform our own lives as well. People often strive to serve and imitate good leaders, and in the Lord we have the best leader of all. We should always try to serve the Lord well.

Prayer: *Dear God, thank you for equipping us and using us to build up others. Guide us to imitate you in all that we do. Amen.*

Thought for the day: When I serve Jesus, no act of kindness is too small.

Mark A. Carter (Oregon, USA)

Our greatest hope

Read Romans 12:9–21

Be joyful in hope, patient in affliction, faithful in prayer.
Romans 12:12 (NIV)

Learning about all the injustices around us and throughout the world can lead us to question our own humanity. Today specifically I prayed about two serious global situations: the suffering caused by the war in Ukraine and the repressive, brutal treatment women endure in some societies. We live in a time of uncertainty and anguish. Is it possible that we are ignoring completely that each of us was created by the mighty hand of God and for God's glory?

Stubbornness, lies and arrogance distract us from God's divine plan and cause us to overlook the suffering of others. But the Lord is our one true source, on whom we can rely. And so our greatest hope is to persevere in word and deed – prayer and action – asking God to forgive and renew us by the Holy Spirit so that we may be in harmony with God and in harmony with all God's people.

Prayer: *Dear God, cause the Holy Spirit to move in us and through us to confront injustices and work to honour you, our rock and our strength. Amen.*

Thought for the day: Today I will keep striving to honour God.

Martha C. Ramírez (Colombia)

A long Good Friday

Read Romans 5:1–5

Hope does not put us to shame, because God's love has been poured into our hearts through the Holy Spirit that has been given to us.
Romans 5:5 (NRSV)

On the evening of Good Friday 2023, I was infected with Covid-19 for the first time since the pandemic began. As a retired cleric, I was due to cover an Easter morning Communion service for another parish, have friends around for Easter lunch, and then give holiday cover over the Easter week for some clergy. So the next day, as the virus took hold, I had to contact people to cancel these commitments. It then took me several weeks to fully recover from the disease. It was my strangest Easter since 2020, when everything was abruptly shut down.

That Easter week also coincided with the 25th anniversary of the Good Friday/Belfast Agreement, which brought dramatic change to the political situation in Northern Ireland. Growing up through the Troubles and living through the run up to this agreement, I remember well that long Good Friday of final negotiations and the hope that came in the wake of the agreement. It was not a perfect deal; no human arrangement can be, and there have been many bumps on the road to peace. But it did bring a transformation for a new generation who could grow up in a different atmosphere from that which we older people knew for 30 years.

As I reflected on both my personal brush with Covid and my country's continuing struggle towards stability, I recognised that some Good Fridays can seem longer than others. But in our faith there is always the promise of Easter Day and the hope of resurrection and restoration.

Prayer: *Father God, thank you that whatever life brings us, through the resurrection of Jesus you give us hope. Amen.*

Thought for the day: God will never abandon me.

Mercia Flanagan (Northern Ireland, United Kingdom)

Holy Saturday

Read John 19:38–42

After these things, Joseph of Arimathea, who was a disciple of Jesus, though a secret one because of his fear of the Jews, asked Pilate to let him take away the body of Jesus. Pilate gave him permission, so he came and removed his body.

John 19:38 (NRSV)

Holy Saturday is a day of quiet, sombre reflection. It's an odd, in-between day after Jesus' death but before his resurrection. I often think about what the day might have been like for the disciples and others who followed Jesus at the time – particularly Joseph of Arimathea.

Joseph had a lot of influence and was an important Jewish leader. He would risk his reputation and standing in the community if his belief in Jesus became public. So he kept his belief quiet.

But on Good Friday, when Jesus died on the cross, Joseph of Arimathea proclaimed his faith publicly by going to Pilate and asking for Jesus' body so he could bury it.

I imagine Joseph spending most of Saturday wondering if he had made the right choice. He took a great risk with this act. And on Saturday, Jesus was still dead in a tomb.

In a similar way, we take risks when we choose to follow Jesus publicly. Those risks can sometimes cause us to stay quiet or to keep our belief secret. However, while making our faith public may make for an uncomfortable Holy Saturday, it makes for a much more celebratory Easter Sunday.

Prayer: *Dear Jesus, help us not to hide our faith but to follow you boldly. Amen.*

Thought for the day: I will express my faith in Jesus openly today.

Trevor Lovell (Utah, USA)

Easter Sunday

Read Matthew 28:1–10

After the Sabbath, as the first day of the week was dawning, Mary Magdalene and the other Mary went to see the tomb.
Matthew 28:1 (NRSV)

Now that I am retired, I have the chance to more closely observe nature as part of my morning routine. At sunrise in the Sonoran Desert of the southwest United States, I've observed lizards warming themselves on rocks so they can start their days with speed and agility. I've observed buzzards perched on tall saguaro cacti to warm their wings before they soar overhead. I've watched my old dog nap in the warmth of the morning sun to soothe his stiff joints.

When I read today's scripture passage, I ask myself, 'What motivated these women to venture out at dawn to anoint the broken body of the crucified Jesus?' I believe these faithful women were driven to action not only by Jewish custom but also by the promise of the resurrected Christ and the hope that is offered in the sunrise of the new day.

Many congregations around the world celebrate Easter morning with a sunrise service of worship – a celebration of our belief in the risen Messiah. So, in addition to warmth and comfort, the sunrise also offers us hope. We join together with other Christians with a shout of 'He is risen!' and embrace the hope that is offered with each new sunrise.

Prayer: *Resurrecting God, thank you for the sunrise of Easter morning. Strengthen our faith so that we are able to meet each new sunrise with the hope offered by our risen Lord. In Jesus' name we pray. Amen.*

Thought for the day: There is hope in the sunrise of each new day.

Doug Wingert (Arizona, USA)

Go anyway

Read Mark 16:1–8

Trust in the Lord with all your heart and lean not on your own understanding.
Proverbs 3:5 (NIV)

As I was reading through the story of Christ's resurrection in Mark 16, something caught my eye. Mary Magdalene, Mary the mother of James and Salome were on their way to the tomb to anoint Jesus' body. Verse 3 makes it clear that they didn't know who would move the stone away from the tomb's entrance so that they could perform their task. And yet these women went anyway, and they were the first people to learn of the glorious news of Christ's resurrection. What a privilege!

I thought about all the times I have felt God leading me to do something, only to hesitate, convincing myself that I wouldn't succeed because of some obstacle I could not overcome on my own. How often have I left things undone due to my hesitation? How many blessings have I missed by not stepping forward in faith and trusting God to provide the help I need?

Years ago, when I was leaving my hometown for a job with a ministry in another state, friends gave me a plaque that reads, 'The will of God will never lead you where the grace of God cannot keep you.' I pray that I may keep those words and the example of the women in Mark's gospel in mind when I feel God's leading in the future and that despite any uncertainty I may feel, I will go anyway.

Prayer: *Heavenly Father, help me depend on your guidance rather than my own understanding. Amen.*

Thought for the day: I will trust God and step forward in faith.

Lisa Stackpole (Wisconsin, USA)

The plank

Read Matthew 7:1–5

You, therefore, have no excuse, you who pass judgment on someone else, for at whatever point you judge another, you are condemning yourself, because you who pass judgment do the same things.
Romans 2:1 (NIV)

I recently underwent surgery on both eyes. While the surgery was successful, it did leave me for a short time with an aggravating sharp irritation in one eye. It was during those couple of weeks that I felt God was reminding me of Jesus' words in today's reading.

I have a tendency to judge a person on first sight – forming an opinion about them based on their appearance, speech or mannerisms before getting to know them. I have lost count of the number of times that I have prejudged someone only to find, to my shame, that the person is a far cry from my initial impression, resulting in many blessings.

Just like the physical surgery I underwent, I need spiritual surgery to remove the 'plank' from my eye. Through God's grace and teaching this can be achieved.

Prayer: *Heavenly Father, you created us in your good and perfect image. Help us to be more like Jesus and see those we come into contact with through his eyes and not through our narrow first impression. Amen.*

Thought for the day: 'Mercy triumphs over judgment' (James 2:13).

John Hauselman (England, United Kingdom)

The project

Read 2 Kings 19:1–19

Hezekiah trusted in the Lord, the God of Israel. There was no one like him among all the kings of Judah, either before him or after him.
2 Kings 18:5 (NIV)

'Mummy, it's growing!' my young daughter exclaimed. 'Let me see,' I said, grabbing the plastic cup from her hands. I was amazed. The maize seed we had been watering for weeks had finally germinated. It was a school project she was due to submit the following week. I had given up hope after eight days and was planning on dumping the whole thing into the trash that morning. I even once said to her, 'It's a useless waste of time and water', to which she replied confidently, 'My teacher says it will grow.' And it sure did. No wonder Jesus says in Luke 18:16 that we must have childlike faith.

My daughter trusted in her teacher's words and kept on watering the soil long after I had given up. In the same way God wants us to hold on to faith even when we're discouraged by the current situation.

King Hezekiah was on the verge of despair when he received a second threat in writing from the Assyrian king, even though God had assured him of deliverance. To quell his despondence, he told God about it personally, and God delivered him and the whole of Jerusalem. So like King Hezekiah, let us continue trusting in the word of the Lord, for God is always faithful.

Prayer: *Dear God, may our confidence in your word be steadfast. Amen.*

Thought for the day: God is always faithful.

Catherine Kwao (Greater Accra Region, Ghana)

Peacemakers

Read Matthew 5:1–12

Blessed are the peacemakers, for they will be called children of God.
Matthew 5:9 (NIV)

We will all socialise with different groups during our lifetime – family, church members, neighbours, coworkers and other groups. When we fellowship with others, we often want them to embrace our opinions and ideas. But this attitude causes a lot of problems and conflict. If we all could develop a sense of openness to hearing others' points of view and opinions, we would have more peaceful fellowship and dialogue in our world.

As I have grown older, I have come to believe that it is our job as good neighbours to listen to and embrace others as much as possible. Jesus exhorts us to be peacemakers in our interactions and relationships. So let us all try to be peacemakers as much as possible. As Galatians 6:9 says: 'Let us not become weary in doing good, for at the proper time we will reap a harvest if we do not give up.'

Prayer: *God of peace, help us to be better peacemakers in the world. Give us a sense of openness towards the people we meet. We pray as Jesus taught us: 'Our Father which art in heaven, Hallowed be thy name. Thy kingdom come. Thy will be done, as in heaven, so in earth. Give us day by day our daily bread. And forgive us our sins; for we also forgive every one that is indebted to us. And lead us not into temptation; but deliver us from evil' (Luke 11:2–4, KJV). Amen.*

Thought for the day: Today I will remain open to listening to and embracing others.

Hugh J. Johnson Jr. (Texas, USA)

Storms in life

Read Mark 9:14–29

Cast your burden on the Lord – he will support you! God will never let the righteous be shaken!
Psalm 55:22 (CEB)

'My legs feel numb, Mum,' exclaimed my 14-year-old daughter. 'They have felt numb for the past month.' The diagnosis was multiple sclerosis – a neurological disease involving the nervous system. Periods of blindness and loss of mobility were difficult to endure for a young girl who enjoyed an active life. Steroids were effective but came with side effects.

As a widowed mother, I felt alone and forlorn. My dreams for my daughter seemed to crumble before me. However, my daughter maintained her zeal for life and continued to live each day with a cheerful smile. She accepted her diagnosis more quickly than I did.

I soon realised that only Christ could replace my desperation with peace. God has not promised us a life free from stress and worry, but God will never leave us. When we bring our worries to God and trust that God can carry us through life's storms, our joy need not fluctuate with our circumstances. God is waiting for us to hand our worries over so that we can find peace.

Prayer: *Dear Lord, help us to rejoice and to trust you in all circumstances. Amen.*

Thought for the day: When I face turbulent waters, God never leaves nor forsakes me.

Sylvia Engen Espe (Alberta, Canada)

PRAYER FOCUS: PARENTS STRUGGLING WITH A CHILD'S DIAGNOSIS

Strength to continue

Read Joshua 1:7–9

This book of the law shall not depart out of your mouth; you shall meditate on it day and night, so that you may be careful to act in accordance with all that is written in it. For then you shall make your way prosperous, and then you shall be successful.

Joshua 1:8 (NRSV)

My first bicycle was a black Mongoose with silver trim. I remember the sheer exhilaration of riding my bike as a child and the freedom it offered. But there was an obstacle: I was still on training wheels. After many, many attempts at learning to ride without training wheels, I quit. For decades, being unable to ride a bicycle remained a source of shame, regret and embarrassment for me.

In my 30s, my wife was training for a marathon. I wanted to be with her while she trained, so I revisited my old nemesis. Within one hour, armed with newfound knowledge thanks to YouTube, I was riding a bike. It's remarkable what obstacles we can overcome when we approach them with determination and wisdom.

Our life in Christ is much the same. No matter how much time we spend with Jesus praying, meditating on scripture or worshipping, we still need to bring effort to the task. Likewise, no matter how hard we try, we can't overcome obstacles without the wisdom offered to us by Christ. When our God-given tenacity comes together with the wisdom and presence of God found in the practice of spiritual disciplines, we can succeed.

Prayer: *God of transformation, draw us into your heart and lead us to be transformed by your presence. Amen.*

Thought for the day: When I rely on God, I receive strength and wisdom from God.

Robert A. Perales (Texas, USA)

Picture perfect

Read Psalm 139:13–18

You created my inmost being; you knit me together in my mother's womb. I praise you because I am fearfully and wonderfully made; your works are wonderful, I know that full well.

Psalm 139:13–14 (NIV)

I am in the process of publishing my first book. It's about my experiences of being bullied as a child because I stutter. A picture of myself and my bio will be on the back cover. A handful of questions buzz around in my head. How should I style my hair? Should I smile or look slightly serious? What should I wear? What should I say about myself? All these questions will be answered in due time. But one thing is for sure: No matter how much I doll myself up, I will still be me – Rachel. Rachel the curious, Rachel the impulsive and Rachel the child of God.

When God looks at me, God doesn't see all my imperfections but sees someone created with intricate talents and abilities. Psalm 139:13–14 says: 'You created my inmost being, you knit me together in my mother's womb. I praise you because I am fearfully and wonderfully made.' God thinks we are beautiful no matter what others may think.

When we look in the mirror, we can remember that we are seeing God's picture-perfect work of art.

Prayer: *Dear God, remind us that we are your works of art, and forgive us when we fail to see the unique beauty in ourselves and others. Amen.*

Thought for the day: All that God creates is worthy of my praise.

Rachel E. Dancy (Michigan, USA)

In the storm

Read Matthew 8:23–27

Do not fear, for I am with you; do not be afraid, for I am your God; I will strengthen you; I will help you; I will uphold you with my victorious right hand.
Isaiah 41:10 (NRSV)

I was only a year old when my family migrated from East Pakistan (now Bangladesh) to West Bengal, India. As refugees, we lived in a tent provided by the government for over seven years. I remember one hot summer evening a heavy storm was developing. We were playing in an open field, and my older sister became worried and brought us back to our tent for safety.

As soon as we got back, the wind was so forceful that we worried we would lose our tent and all our belongings. Imagining what it would be like to lose our tent and be without a place to live, I started praying to God. I felt that my prayer was not working. But then I started to talk to Jesus. I started pleading with Jesus: *We don't have another tent. If this one is gone, where shall we live?* I was at the corner of our tent holding the rope when I cried, 'Help me, Jesus!' To my amazement, the wind gradually weakened and finally disappeared.

This experience has had a lasting impact on my life. God hears us when we call out for help. Truly Jesus is with us in every storm.

Prayer: *Dear God, thank you for being with us even when we go through difficult times in life. In Jesus' name. Amen.*

Thought for the day: Jesus is with me in every storm.

Subodh C. Mondal (Delhi, India)

Ten people prayed

Read 1 Corinthians 12:12–20

*They devoted themselves to the apostles' teaching and to fellowship,
to the breaking of bread and to prayer.*
Acts 2:42 (NIV)

A few years ago, I felt like something was missing from my life. My days lacked meaning and purpose. However, instead of bringing my concern to God, I looked for fulfilment in lots of wrong places – which only left me feeling emptier. But I struggled to change my ways and turn to God.

My church group was focusing on spiritual health and encouraged members to share their struggles. At first I was hesitant to discuss my emptiness. Most people value strength, independence and success, not fragility or need. But I finally opened up to the group and asked for help.

After that meeting, ten people started praying for me. Soon after, I sensed God's presence and power in the circumstances around me, steering me away from distractions. Sermons, devotionals and Bible verses reminded me of God's provision. Together, these factors helped me look to God.

Being vulnerable wasn't easy. But when I asked, I found that others were glad to help. Group members checked in on me regularly and offered encouragement. Their prayers and God's responses gave me hope that God would give me new purpose and supply what was missing from my life.

Prayer: *Thank you, God, for responding to the prayers of our church family. Help us to ask for support when we need it. Amen.*

Thought for the day: When I need help, I will reach out to others.

Jennifer Kirsch (Ohio, USA)

Are you sure, Lord?

Read John 4:4–24

God is in that city. It will never crumble. God will help it when morning dawns.
Psalm 46:5 (CEB)

I can remember the phone call like it was yesterday. My house was a disaster with laundry everywhere and dishes to put away. One of my daughters was angry with me and had just hung up the phone abruptly. Even the dog was unhappy with me that day. I was feeling like a failure.

The district church leaders put me on speaker phone and asked if I would be willing to serve as the regional lay leader for the next four years, and my response was, 'Are you sure you want *me* to do this?' In that moment, I didn't feel successful at my own life, much less worthy to serve on that level. How powerful it was for me to know that, as messy as I was, they saw God at work in my life. I thought of the woman at the well and how so many would not have wanted her to be the poster child for Christ. Yet, she perfectly represents those of us who follow Christ.

If we want to grow the church and bring hearts to Christ, we need to believe that all hearts are worthy. We need to believe that our own hearts are worthy of sharing the hope of his love with others. One year into my service, I don't try to hide my messy and imperfect life. I openly share it with others. I want others who are struggling to know that they are not alone. We are in this together with Christ.

Prayer: *Gracious and loving God, help us to follow where you lead with humility and honesty so that others will know faith is a journey for us all. Amen.*

Thought for the day: God knows me and loves me anyway.

Kimberly Rice Smith (North Carolina, USA)

Small gifts

Read Luke 11:1–13

Every good and perfect gift is from above, coming down from the Father of the heavenly lights, who does not change like shifting shadows.
James 1:17 (NIV)

When I retired four years ago, I was given a small, round, handsewn cushion. I kept it on a chair, mainly for ornamental reasons. However, recently the cushion has become useful for me every day.

For the past two months I've been recovering from spinal decompression surgery. Sleep has been difficult due to the uncomfortable surgical wound in my lower back. When I was urged by my physiotherapist to place a pillow or cushion between my knees while sleeping, I suddenly remembered the gift of the small cushion and began using it as prescribed. Imagine my delight to find that the cushion helped me sleep virtually pain-free!

Our loving God gives us gifts each day – gifts we often don't even recognise, let alone use. But the Bible is filled with accounts of our caring God providing gifts to so many people – the best example being the gift of God's Son, Jesus Christ! The gift of a small cushion has reawakened my discovery of the big and small gifts God gives us each and every day.

Prayer: *Loving God, thank you for the gift of Jesus Christ and the many gifts you provide each day. Amen.*

Thought for the day: What gifts has God provided me today?

Roland Rink (Gauteng, South Africa)

Hands and feet

Read Matthew 25:31–40

Jesus said, 'Truly I tell you, whatever you did for one of the least of these brothers and sisters of mine, you did for me.'
Matthew 25:40 (NIV)

Today's scripture reading means the world to me. This passage helped me to realise that Jesus wants us to be his hands and feet.

I have found different ways to honour Christ through acts of service. Some years back, I began visiting a 94-year-old woman in a local nursing home every Wednesday. I found joy in hearing her talk about cooking on a wood-burning stove and other memories from her younger days. She went to be with Jesus at age 96. Now I help with our church's food ministry. We give food to those in need and also make coffee at the church on Sunday mornings. I enjoy smiling, hugging people and saying, 'Good morning!'

There is always a need that can be met. You might volunteer at the hospital, drive someone to a doctor's appointment or send a birthday card to a church member. Even holding a door open for someone can be a way to serve Christ. We bless others with each act of service, and we are blessed as well when we honour Jesus with our hands and feet.

Prayer: *Dear God, thank you for allowing us to be your hands and feet. In Jesus' name, we pray. Amen.*

Thought for the day: Today I can be the hands and feet of Christ.

Roxie Ewing (Alabama, USA)

Acceptance

Read John 8:1–11

Jesus straightened up and asked her, 'Woman, where are they? Has no one condemned you?' 'No one, sir,' she said. 'Then neither do I condemn you,' Jesus declared. 'Go now and leave your life of sin.'
John 8:10–11 (NIV)

Jesus' ministry challenges us to accept people in spite of their flaws and imperfections. When Jesus began his ministry, he encountered different kinds of people. Many liked and loved him and his teachings, but some did not accept him or his teachings.

When a woman caught in adultery was brought before him, Jesus did not judge or condemn her. Jesus did not avoid her or look down on her. Jesus did not hate her. Jesus did something unexpected. He accepted the woman – in spite of her sin and social status.

Regardless of our mistakes and sins, acceptance is what we all need. Jesus shows us that acceptance is possible even when people are different from one another or hold different points of view. We can give the gift of acceptance to others because God has accepted us.

Prayer: *Father God, thank you for accepting us. Please help us to accept others. Amen.*

Thought for the day: I follow Jesus' example when I accept others as they are.

Golda Dilema (Cavite, Philippines)

An army of helpers

Read 1 John 3:16–18

Carry each other's burdens, and in this way you will fulfil the law of Christ.
Galatians 6:2 (NIV)

Several years ago, a close family friend and brother in Christ was diagnosed with stage-four colon cancer. Along with the diagnosis came a multitude of concerns. Our friend was the principal breadwinner, so how long could he work to support his family? It was a frightening time.

The apostle Paul admonished the church in Galatia to bear one another's burdens. Through our friend's long struggle with cancer, God taught me and others the true meaning of Paul's words. To carry another's burden, we must sacrifice something, whether time, energy or money. Some families combined resources to pay our friend's rent and bills. Some gave gift cards for groceries. Some volunteered to drive him back and forth to chemotherapy appointments. A veritable army of helpers stepped up to bear this family's burdens. Above all, we were in constant prayer for our friend's healing.

We also learned that when God calls us to bear one another's burdens, it doesn't mean that we must carry all of it alone; we only need to carry the piece we are given. My piece might not look like your piece. But if we each carry our part, then it lessens the overall load. In carrying others' burdens, we fulfil the law of Christ – to love one another as God has loved us.

Prayer: *Dear Jesus, teach us how to love others as you love us. Help us to bear the burdens of others with compassion. Amen.*

Thought for the day: I show God's love by bearing others' burdens.

Daphne Goodman (Maryland, USA)

A safe place

Read Psalm 138

When they call to me, I will answer them; I will be with them in trouble; I will rescue them and honour them.
Psalm 91:15 (NRSV)

In the 1950s I attended a boarding school for boys. It was run in a military style with strict discipline and punishments that were often issued in an abusive manner. Bullying at the school was rampant and persistent. Needless to say, I suffered at the school and learned how to avoid any confrontation, disappearing into anonymity when required.

One place in my school that nobody went during the day was the chapel. There I found my retreat where solace and support awaited me. I found that I was not alone. I felt God's reassuring presence, and I enjoyed that calming influence and support. This was the beginning of my lifelong journey with God.

I still give thanks to God for coming into my life. I cannot give thanks for the experience of being bullied, but I am grateful that during that time I found God. What might my life have become without that sacred introduction?

Prayer: *Loving God, please cleanse the hearts and minds of those who abuse others. Be with those facing persecution, and grant us lives of harmony and peace. Amen.*

Thought for the day: In God, I can find peace, reassurance and protection.

Johannes von Buch (Nigeria)

Who are my children?

Read Isaiah 54:1–8

*'Bring my sons from afar and my daughters from the ends
of the earth.'*
Isaiah 43:6 (NIV)

My husband and I were happily married for 48 years, but we were never able to have children.

Recently reading Isaiah 54, I was challenged to ask myself, 'So who are my children?' I was led to conclude that if, as it says in verse 5, 'your Maker is your husband', then his children are mine. I therefore have a responsibility to God's children everywhere. I do not know each one individually, but he does.

Of course, I cannot meet the needs of everyone, but if I let God guide me, then he will ensure that I can meet, serve and help those who need me most. This is definitely a voyage of discovery, and I do not know where it will lead me, but I can follow where God leads me knowing that his way is good.

Prayer: *Dear Lord, help me to follow in your steps and care for your children wherever they are. We pray the prayer you taught us, 'Father, hallowed be your name, your kingdom come. Give us each day our daily bread. Forgive us our sins, for we also forgive everyone who sins against us. And lead us not into temptation' (Luke 11:2–4, NIV). Amen.*

Thought for the day: We are all God's children (see Acts 17:28).

Hilary Hartley (England, United Kingdom)

Anchored

Read Psalm 46

We have this hope as an anchor for the soul, firm and secure.
Hebrews 6:19 (NIV)

My husband Mike and I were visiting a nearby town for our routine eye examinations. As we looked at the array of new frames, Mike suddenly fainted, hitting his head on the floor. Although he came around fairly quickly, he was clearly shaken and had a huge bump on his head. We called an ambulance and made our way to the hospital.

As we waited in a crowded corridor, I found myself wondering where God was. *Why had this happened? What damage had been done?* If only I could feel God's peace instead of feeling stressed.

Then something came to mind from the devotional I had read that morning. To be honest, I couldn't remember many details; but I knew it was something about anchors: how St Paul was tossed around in a ship at sea and how God holds us secure in the storms of life. How appropriate!

I felt that God was saying to me, 'I am holding you. You are anchored.' I kept repeating this to myself through the time of anxious waiting at the hospital. I didn't feel a warm glow of peace, but I knew that we were in God's hands. We were anchored.

And Mike was and is okay. I give thanks for God's faithfulness and for God's word that still speaks to us today.

Prayer: *Thank you, faithful God, that when the storms of life shake our security you hold us and never let us go. Amen.*

Thought for the day: I am anchored in God's love.

April McIntyre (England, United Kingdom)

Waving at the window

Read Revelation 3:14–21

'Here I am! I stand at the door and knock.'
Revelation 3:20 (NIV)

I always had the duty of dropping our kids off at daycare, which is more emotionally difficult than my husband's duty of picking them up. My children didn't like being left, and many mornings were filled with tears. It also didn't help that our daycare was across town from where I worked, so I was inevitably always in a rush.

One morning, I was rushing out of the daycare to my car, when something caught my eye. In a window facing the parking lot stood my two-year-old son waving excitedly at me. It was a sweet gesture and just what I needed. I told everyone at work how sweet my son was.

The next morning, when dropping my son off, I mentioned to the teacher how my son had made me smile the day before. She kindly told me that he does that every morning and had been doing so for months. My heart sank. I never missed his wave after that.

This experience made me wonder how many times I have missed signs of God's love because I was too rushed to notice. Praise the Lord we are loved by a God who is patient and whose love never ends.

Prayer: *Dear God, forgive us when we don't notice all the ways you love us. Thank you for patiently waiting on us and for loving us unconditionally. Amen.*

Thought for the day: I will look for glimpses of God's love for me today.

Rebekah L. Callen (Texas, USA)

Listening to God

Read 1 Peter 5:1–10

Humble yourselves, therefore, under God's mighty hand, that he may lift you up in due time. Cast all your anxiety on him because he cares for you.
1 Peter 5:6–7 (NIV)

I had a good job, a family and a house in the suburbs. Then I got divorced and everything changed. Living in my car on a noisy city street, sleeping with a blanket over my head to keep out the cold and city lights, and eating alone on a bench in the park forced me to reflect and listen to God.

I was welcomed by others in the homeless community, and their acceptance helped me see that God is in every person, maybe especially in the homeless one. Homelessness was humbling, but Jesus humbled himself for us. We are called to walk humbly with God, just as Jesus did on his way to the cross. God eventually lifted me up, teaching me to cast away my worries, to see God in nature, to value every person and to leave my life in God's hands.

God directed me to a church community that has helped me grow in faith, where I work on outreach missions, including with those who are homeless. The support of the people in this community has made it easier to follow God's way. God calls us to feed the hungry, visit the sick, welcome the stranger and care for the homeless. Listen.

Prayer: *Open our eyes and hearts, O God, to the needs of those around us. Open our ears to listen to your promptings. Amen.*

Thought for the day: God leads me through every circumstance to help me reach my calling.

Brian Rogers (Massachusetts, USA)

The power of salt

Read Colossians 4:2–6

Let your conversation be always full of grace, seasoned with salt, so that you may know how to answer everyone.
Colossians 4:6 (NIV)

Families from our church who live in the neighbourhood are part of the neighbourhood fellowship group. We meet every month for Bible study, prayer and to catch up on our families' welfare. It is a time of fellowship and community building. We always bring food to share. On one occasion I made some chicken curry for the dinner. I expected to receive some compliments for it, but no one said anything. Finally, I asked if they liked the dish. They looked at each other without responding to me. Wondering what the matter was, I took a spoonful of it to taste. To my horror I found it to be tasteless. I had forgotten to add salt!

I was reminded of Jesus' words in Matthew 5:13: 'You are the salt of the earth. But if the salt loses its saltiness, how can it be made salty again? It is no longer good for anything, except to be thrown out and trampled underfoot.' As salt of the earth, we work to preserve all that is good and just in the world by being peacemakers and peacekeepers. Just as salt adds flavour to food, as Christians we can bring love, kindness and grace to those around us in partnership with God, reflecting God's love and light in the world.

Prayer: *Loving God, we long to serve you. Help us to build a just and peaceful society where we reflect your love and compassion to those around us. Amen.*

Thought for the day: Jesus calls me to bring God's love and light to the world.

Navamani Peter (Karnataka, India)

Praying boldly

Read Matthew 18:1–5

Jesus said, 'Truly I tell you, unless you change and become like little children, you will never enter the kingdom of heaven.'
Matthew 18:3 (NIV)

Our young daughter was tucked into bed, covers up to her chin. After a song, I asked her the same question we pose every evening: 'What do you want to pray about?'

She paused, lips pursed together, forehead furrowed in thought. Her sweet toddler voice responded, 'I want to ask God to make unicorns real.'

In the hardships of daily life, it's not difficult to lose our joyful, trusting, wide-eyed faith. But as for children, why wouldn't they ask God for anything? If God can heal the sick, raise the dead and create the planets in outer space, surely God can make unicorns real! And if my daughter has faith enough to pray for that, I want a childlike faith to ask God for big, bold things too.

We all experience times when our faith feels small, when we haven't dared to hope that God can bring healing or reconciliation or fulfilment. Even then, God is still the God of the impossible. So let's take a page from the children among us and start asking God for the big, seemingly impossible things.

Prayer: *Dear God, inspire our doubting hearts to believe and trust you with childlike faith. Give us audacity to pray boldly. In the name of Jesus. Amen!*

Thought for the day: Today I will pray boldly.

Gretchen Schloesser (Arizona, USA)

Hall of mirrors

Read Genesis 1:26–31

For we are God's handiwork, created in Christ Jesus to do good works, which God prepared in advance for us to do.
Ephesians 2:10 (NIV)

Have you ever walked through a hall of mirrors at a fairground? Each mirror you stand in front of distorts your image. What is reflected back is a caricature of what you really look like – you can appear to be very thin and long, very wide and short or anything in between!

Sometimes I can live my life as though I am in a hall of mirrors, judging myself based on what I see reflected back to me by others, perhaps their opinions of me or things they have said or not said. The world can be pretty good at reflecting back to us a distorted image of what we are worth, based on our wealth, status or qualifications. Sometimes these reflections can lead us to have a harsh and unkind image of ourselves, or perhaps even an over-inflated sense of our own importance.

The creation story in Genesis 1 reminds us that we are image bearers of Christ. We are all unique, handmade and original. We are able to think, relate, choose and feel as God designed us to and also to love and be loved. Sometimes it can take time to see ourselves differently, and it can be a struggle, but Ephesians 2:10 reminds us that we are God's 'handiwork'; we are his masterpiece. That is the real truth about us.

Prayer: *Lord, help us today to see ourselves as you see us, not according to what the world or others say. Thank you that we are your handiwork.*

Thought for the day: I am an image bearer of Christ, an original masterpiece.

Caroline Mansell (England, United Kingdom)

Despite, not because

Read 1 Thessalonians 5:12–18

Give thanks in all circumstances.
1 Thessalonians 5:18 (NIV)

I have often heard it said that God will never give us more than we can handle. Yet, there are times in our lives when this is simply not true, and such statements ring hollow. Perhaps the biblical passages used to promote this idea have been misinterpreted. For example, 1 Corinthians 10:13 is a verse commonly cited, but it is about temptation rather than suffering.

Passages like 1 Thessalonians 5:16–18 and James 1:2 tell us to rejoice always. But being told to rejoice when we have lost a loved one or are facing a life-altering health diagnosis can seem cruel. The command to rejoice in our suffering, however, is about rejoicing in Jesus *despite* our circumstances, not *because of* our circumstances. What a difference that understanding can make when trials come! It is much easier to rejoice in Jesus and what he has done for us than to rejoice in the difficulties we face.

Understanding these passages better has helped me lift my gaze from dire situations to God, who is with us every step of the way, offering hope, joy and encouragement in the midst of life's most difficult circumstances.

Prayer: *Heavenly Father, thank you for being with us in our suffering. Help us to rejoice in you despite not because of our circumstances. In the name of Jesus we pray. Amen.*

Thought for the day: Is my gaze focused on God or my circumstances?

Bronwyn Ashton Winch (Queensland, Australia)

God provides strength

Read Hebrews 12:1–11

Consider him who endured such opposition from sinners, so that you will not grow weary and lose heart.

Hebrews 12:3 (NIV)

I loved coaching the eight-year-old Rangers Little League team. They learned an important life lesson during the season-ending tournament. The Rangers had yet to win a game, and the team and their parents couldn't wait for the season to be over.

Fully expecting to lose, we played our first game of the tournament and won. The next day, we won again. The third game was against the best team in the league. They had dominated the league all season. Our team said, 'We don't stand a chance.' But I told them anything is possible and this is why we play the game. We won the final game by a landslide.

As I contemplate the lesson the Rangers learned that day, I am reminded of our passage in Hebrews where we are instructed to run the race that has been marked for us. Although we face opposition, we are surrounded by a cloud of witnesses and should not grow weary in our efforts. We must never give up or lose heart. When we face challenges that seem insurmountable, we need only to place our focus on God and God's promises. Our God will provide the strength we need for what lies ahead.

Prayer: *Dear God, as we run our race, help us to fix our eyes on you and not grow weary. Amen.*

Thought for the day: When I focus on God, I will not grow weary.

Steve Wakefield (Alabama, USA)

Guiding light

Read John 16:1–15

'I have told you these things, so that in me you may have peace. In this world you will have trouble. But take heart! I have overcome the world.'
John 16:33 (NIV)

Watching the sunrise from my balcony is something I always await with enthusiasm. One day I was disappointed because there were many dark, thick clouds in the sky. I thought it would certainly begin to rain soon, but slowly the dark clouds turned red. As time passed, the clouds began to dissipate until finally the sun shone brightly. Hardly believing what I had just seen, I realised that like the light of the sun overcoming the dark clouds that morning, God is greater than all my problems.

Sometimes life feels gloomy and we just live day by day without a clear sense of purpose. However, when we trust in Jesus, he is the light that guides our way and with his strength we do not carry our burdens alone. Jesus gives us the Holy Spirit to direct our steps so that we can always move forward with hope.

Prayer: *Triune God, life is full of uncertainty, yet we know we can rely on you. Comfort us during hard times, and help us to look forward in hope to the promise of salvation. Amen.*

Thought for the day: I will look for the light of Christ to guide me.

Kumalawaty Sundari (Jakarta, Indonesia)

PRAYER FOCUS: SOMEONE SEEKING A SENSE OF PURPOSE

The pilgrim's way

Read Psalm 121

*I lift up my eyes to the mountains – where does my help come from?
My help comes from the Lord, the Maker of heaven and earth.*
Psalm 121:1 (NIV)

There are some days, for all of us, when life just feels hard. I was having one of those days, feeling overwhelmed by the demands of family and work life, saddened by events in my community and anxious when I listened to the news. I was at a point of sheer exasperation, wishing I could handle it all better, when a song came on the radio and brought to mind this beautiful psalm.

It is a psalm written for pilgrimage, and as I read it, I picture those Jewish pilgrims with a long, treacherous road ahead of them. I imagine them as they look up at that mountainous path, daunted, but also hope-filled. The journey ahead would be difficult, but also holy.

When making a pilgrimage, the challenge and sacrifice faced help to set the journey apart from other journeys. Each step can be an act of love and worship. There can be great joy in the prospect of drawing nearer to the special place to which you are headed.

Pilgrimages have always been a great metaphor for own lives, in which our challenges can feel like mountains, we can feel tired and overwhelmed and we can worry about the unknowns along our path. Yet, with each step we take, we can trust in God's help.

Prayer: *Lord, thank you that although the road ahead may be difficult, we can trust in your help and love. Amen.*

Thought for the day: God is watching over my coming and going today.

Amy Turner (England, United Kingdom)

Persevering in love

Read Psalm 71:7–18

Do not cast me off in the time of old age; do not forsake me when my strength is spent.
Psalm 71:9 (NRSV)

'The elevator is broken again,' my 93-year-old mother stated for the fourth time during our phone conversation. I contacted her assisted-living facility and learned that the elevator was not broken. The sad truth is that, due to the onset of dementia, she sometimes forgets how to use it.

Over the past two years, I've learned first-hand that having a family member whose memory, perception and reasoning are failing is extremely challenging. Several months ago, after working all day and helping my mother for a few hours in the evening, I felt completely exhausted and tearfully cried out to God, 'I can't keep doing this!' God answered by offering vivid memories of how brilliant, creative, funny, independent and loving my mother had been. This softened my attitude about caring for her. Instead of seeing it only as an exhausting responsibility, I saw the blessing in being able to provide my mother with the same love and support she had selflessly given to me throughout my life.

As her dementia progresses, there continue to be times when caring for my mother is demanding, discouraging and depressing. With God's support, though, I can pause to take a deep breath, whisper a prayer of thanks for having grown up with her as my mother, and persevere in love.

Prayer: *Thank you, God, for the love and support we too often take for granted. Help us to persevere in loving those who need our care. Amen.*

Thought for the day: God is with me even in my most difficult times.

Jill Allen Maisch (Maryland, USA)

Antidote for anger

Read Romans 2:1–11

Do you not realise that God's kindness is meant to lead you to repentance?

Romans 2:4 (NRSV)

I recently experienced an incident that led me to think of and appreciate God's kindness and patience with me. I was angry with a young woman who is under my guardianship. I was even thinking of withdrawing my assistance from her. Yet I knew that if I did, my decision would cut short her education because her parents cannot afford to pay her school fees.

Then one day as I was reading the Bible, I came across words that spoke of God's kindness towards us. I thought of the many times that I have failed God. Yet God has never given up on me. I saw then that I needed to treat this young woman the way God treats me – with kindness and patience.

When we feel provoked by others, we can begin to lose patience with them, even speaking and acting unkindly. But if we remember how the Lord has been kind and patient with us, we can act to bring about reconciliation and peace.

Prayer: *Dear Jesus, help us to exercise the same kindness and patience with others as you so lovingly demonstrated as you walked among us. Give us the courage to follow you faithfully every day. We pray the prayer you taught us, 'Father, hallowed be your name, your kingdom come. Give us each day our daily bread. Forgive us our sins, for we also forgive everyone who sins against us. And lead us not into temptation' (Luke 11:2–4, NIV). Amen.*

Thought for the day: 'A soft answer turns away wrath, but a harsh word stirs up anger' (Proverbs 15:1).

Enid Adah Nyinomujuni (Dar es Salaam, Tanzania)

Perseverance

Read Luke 13:31–35

Jesus cried, 'Jerusalem, Jerusalem!… How often I wanted to gather your people together, just as a hen gathers her chicks under her wings.'
Matthew 23:37 (CEB)

As a young Christian, I committed myself to making the world better first through nursing, then child advocacy, and finally through ordained ministry. Now at the end of my eighth decade, I feel sad that I might die without seeing more of what I had envisioned as the reign of God. I still see injustice all around me. The Covid pandemic revealed global inequities; democracy is threatened around the world; war or threat of war is often present; common civility seems to be in decline.

Jesus had similar feelings of disappointment as he gazed at his beloved Jerusalem. Yet despite warnings from some Pharisees and the threat of death, he did not let this deter him from continuing his healing work.

Seeing Jesus as an example of courage, perseverance and purpose has given me renewed hope that I can still make a difference in my community by remembering my neighbours – near and far – as persons God calls me to love. I pray each day for the strength and courage to do just that.

Prayer: *Holy One, like a mothering hen, keep us safe in your care as we seek to share your love. Amen.*

Thought for the day: Jesus is my guide for how I live my life.

Judy Thomas (Maryland, USA)

Bucket list

Read Psalm 100

Serve the Lord with gladness; come into his presence with singing.
Psalm 100:2 (NRSV)

In recent years, it has become popular for people to make a 'bucket list', a list of things they want to do before they die or 'kick the bucket'. What if we were to make a 'Christian bucket list' – a list of ways we can use our gifts to provide meaningful service for the Lord's work?

I once heard a Christian leader pose the question, 'What makes your heart sing?' I have a number of things on my Christian bucket list that do exactly that. For example, in memory of my late son, I serve on short-term mission teams with an international Christian disability ministry. We deliver and customise wheelchairs for people in need around the world. It brings me much joy to see people experience mobility, many for the first time. It is also a joy to work and worship with other Christians around the world. Writing meditations for Christian resources in hopes that something I share might be helpful to others is another activity that makes my heart sing.

God blesses each of us with skills, interests and experiences that uniquely equip us to serve. When we find ways to serve that draw on those gifts, it can truly make the heart sing.

Prayer: *Dear Lord, thank you for the gifts and talents you give to each person. Help us find ways to serve you joyfully and effectively. In your name. Amen.*

Thought for the day: Joyfully serving the Lord is a blessing.

Darrell Boone (Indiana, USA)

Small group questions

Wednesday 3 January

1 Describe a time when your plans did not work out how you had intended. What other opportunities became possible as a result? How did your life change because of your new plans?

2 When you experience change, do you mourn what you had before? Why or why not? In what ways do you actively nurture a new sense of purpose in such times?

3 Do you believe there are days when nothing important happens? How do you find the significance in what you do every day? How does your focus change how you perceive each day?

4 In what ways do you spend time with God daily? How does this practice affect your behaviour and mood?

5 Do you have a strong sense of purpose and direction? Where does that purpose and direction come from? How does your faith inform your sense of purpose?

Wednesday 10 January

1 How does your faith strengthen and encourage you when you or a loved one is undergoing difficult surgery or treatment? What spiritual practice is most meaningful for you in those times?

2 What role does prayer and devotional reading play in comforting you when you are waiting and hoping for something? How does your practice of prayer and devotional time change depending on your circumstances?

3 Do you find that your prayers are more often requests or expressions of thanksgiving? Why do you think that is? Do you ever wonder if God tires of your requests? Why or why not?

4　What scripture passages remind you of the value of prayer and the way God responds to our prayers? How do these scriptures inform the way you pray?

5　In what ways do your prayerful requests express your faith in God? What do your most recent prayers reveal about your faith?

Wednesday 17 January

1　The cow and calf in today's meditation were vulnerable following the calf's birth. What other instances of vulnerability in nature come to mind for you? What can you learn from those examples?

2　Describe a time when you were surrounded and protected by others. Was the protection you received physical or otherwise? What was that experience like for you?

3　What is the most memorable illustration you have witnessed of God's protection and refuge? Why is that illustration memorable or significant for you?

4　When you are in a difficult or vulnerable situation, do you find it easy to notice the ways God is providing protection and comfort? Why or why not?

5　Where do you find the most refuge and comfort in vulnerable moments? What role does community play in such times? How do you support others in their vulnerable times?

Wednesday 24 January

1　Recall a time when your expectations were not met. Were you disappointed? How did you respond to the situation?

2　Who has given you an unexpected gift? What was the gift? How did you react to their gift? How has that gift impacted you?

3　When you ask God for blessings, do you find yourself hoping for or expecting the same gifts and blessings God gave you before? Why or why not? How often does God give you the same gifts as before?

4 In times when you wish God had given you a different answer to prayer, what scripture verses or spiritual practices help you accept God's answer with open arms? How does your response to God's answers affect your faith and your attitude?

5 Do you find it easy or difficult to anticipate all of God's gifts and blessings with excitement? Why? Who in your life serves as an example for you of excitedly embracing whatever God offers?

Wednesday 31 January

1 When you experience rejection, how does it affect your mood? How do you respond?

2 Have you ever questioned your God-given purpose following a rejection? Why or why not? What strengthens your conviction about your purpose?

3 Recall a time when a rejection served as a catalyst for learning, practice and growth for you. What happened? How did that experience change your path?

4 What activity best allows you to express your love for others and for God? What motivates you to persevere in this activity even when you face obstacles? How does your faith inform your approach to the activity?

5 What does it mean to you that God has weaved within you a divine purpose? What scriptures most remind you of this? How do you answer God's call and purpose for your life each day?

Wednesday 7 February

1 What is the most recent spiritual lesson you have learned from observing nature? Why do you think we so often learn important lessons from creation?

2   Recall a time when you missed an important step in a process and it changed the outcome of a situation. Why was that step so important? What did you learn from this experience?

3   Why do you think daily attention and effort is so important for spiritual growth? In what other areas of your life do you notice the value of daily care and attention?

4   How do you remember to prioritise your spiritual growth each day? How is your life enriched when you spend time with God in this way?

5   Who in your life most encourages you to take time each day to pray and meditate on God's word? What role does your faith community play in your spiritual life?

Wednesday 14 February

1   Have you ever given something up for Lent? Do you find this practice meaningful? Why or why not?

2   Would you ever consider giving up a grudge, anger or resentment for Lent? How do you think that would feel? What do you think might happen?

3   The writer's congregation burned slips of paper to symbolise letting go. Have you ever done something similar? If so, what was your experience? If not, what physical practices help you to let go of something?

4   Why do you think releasing our negative feelings is so freeing? How do you think holding on to those feelings affects us long term?

5   Are you planning to give something up for Lent this year? If so, what will you give up? If not, what other ways do you plan to honour the season of Lent?

Wednesday 21 February

1. Today's writer draws a comparison between spiritual energy and a battery. What image do you feel best represents you and your spiritual energy? Why?

2. When do you notice your spiritual energy is drained the most? What are the biggest drains on your spiritual energy?

3. When do you find your spiritual energy is best replenished? How does the Holy Spirit rejuvenate you? In what ways do you strive to preserve that energy?

4. Do you think distractions lead you away from God? If so, how? If not, what keeps you near to God despite distractions?

5. How can you tell when your spiritual energy is getting low? How does prayer, worship, Bible study and Christian fellowship restore your spiritual energy? What else restores your spiritual energy?

Wednesday 28 February

1. When has fellowship with other Christians provided you comfort and peace during a trying time? Why do you think praying and worshipping with fellow believers can be such a comfort?

2. Have you ever attended worship with a knot of worry inside you? Did the worry fade as you worshipped or did you simply worship in spite of it? What was that experience like?

3. Has anyone ever prayed for you when you didn't have the words to pray? Have you ever prayed for someone who didn't have the words? Describe those experiences.

4. How are you encouraged to know that God hears your cries even before you voice them? What scriptures most remind you of God's constant listening and care?

5. When you know someone in your community is hurting, what do you do? How do you offer them love and support? How does your community do the same for you?

Wednesday 6 March

1 If you give up something for Lent, what do you usually choose? Why? How does that practice affect you during Lent? If you don't give up something, how else do you honour the season of Lent?

2 If you knew you were going to die in 40 days, what would you do? What would you give up? What would you start doing?

3 Have you ever continued a Lenten practice beyond the season of Lent? If so, why? If not, would you ever consider doing so? Why or why not?

4 What would it look like for you to practise Lent every day? How would this change your relationship with God and your relationships with others?

5 What is separating you from God today? What prevents you from letting go of whatever separates you from God? How might letting it go draw you closer to God and help you better follow Christ's leading in your life?

Wednesday 13 March

1 Have you ever had to restart a project partway through? Why did you have to alter your original plan? What was the outcome of the situation?

2 Recall a time when you witnessed a long process. What did you learn from witnessing that process? How did that remind you of the ways God is working in your life?

3 When have you noticed God doing a new thing in your life? In what ways did that new thing change you or your life? How do you remain alert for the ways God is working in you each day?

4 What scriptures remind you most of God's presence and work in your life? Name some spiritual practices that help you remain aware of and open to God's presence. In what ways do these practices bring you closer to God?

5 How can you tell when God is at work in you? In what ways do you proclaim God's great work to others?

Wednesday 20 March

1 Describe a time when you were grateful for light. Why was light so important for you in that moment? What did you learn from that experience?

2 When you are in the dark, do you ever feel scared or helpless? Why or why not? Why do you think a light in the darkness is so comforting and encouraging?

3 How do you think showing kindness to others shares God's light with them? What other behaviours and characteristics help spread God's light among us?

4 Do you find it easy or difficult to keep your light shining when you experience struggles? Why? What helps you to shine God's light in every circumstance?

5 When have you most clearly been shown the light of God through others? How do you strive to shine God's light on those around you? What programmes or ministries in your church or community help shine the light of God to others?

Wednesday 27 March

1 When have you volunteered in a way that allowed you to connect with the people you were serving? How did those relationships enrich your experience? What else enriched your volunteering experience?

2 When you volunteer, do you consider yourself a servant of God or just a volunteer? Why? Does your answer change depending on your circumstances? If so, how?

3 When you think of serving God, what first comes to your mind? Now dig a bit deeper – what other types of service come to mind? What daily actions do you engage in that fit in to these ways of serving?

4 What does it mean to you to live God's words and do God's work? Describe ways you have witnessed transformation as a result of living this way.

5 When have others built you up by serving you? When have you helped build others up through serving them? What could the world look like if more people took time to imitate the Lord and serve others?

Wednesday 3 April

1 Have you ever given up on something only to realise later that it was flourishing? Why did you give up on it? What did you learn from that experience?

2 Why do you think children are able to demonstrate hopeful faith so beautifully? Why do you think adults sometimes struggle to maintain this same type of faith?

3 Do you find it easy or difficult to hold on to hope and faith when you are discouraged or struggling? Why? What spiritual practices, activities or Bible verses help you hold fast even in trying times?

4 Have you ever doubted God or scripture? Why or why not? What helps you continue trusting in God and scripture when doubts creep in?

5 Who in scripture serves as the best example for you of trusting God in the face of adversity? How did they respond to their circumstances? In what ways do you strive to follow their example?

Wednesday 10 April

1 When it seems like everything in your life is a mess, do you ever feel like a failure? Why or why not? What helps you get through such times?

2 When have you been offered an opportunity that you did not expect? What was the situation? What did that experience teach you about yourself and about God?

3 When you feel unworthy to serve God in a certain way, what scripture passages remind you that we are all worthy to serve God? How are you encouraged by those verses?

4 Do you feel like you need to hide the messy and imperfect parts of your life? Why or why not? What happens when you allow others to see those parts of your life?

5 How are you encouraged to know that you are not alone in your struggles? How do you show others that it's okay not to have everything figured out? In what ways do you think this kind of honesty and humility strengthens a faith community?

Wednesday 17 April

1 When you are in the middle of a stressful or unexpected situation, what thoughts run through your mind? Do you easily feel God's peace in those moments? Why or why not?

2 Have you ever wondered where God was in your situation? Did you ultimately find God in the situation? Describe your experience.

3 When do you most clearly feel anchored by God? How does your relationship with God change depending on whether you feel anchored or tossed around as if at sea?

4 Recall a time when remembering a scripture or devotional reading helped you through overwhelming circumstances. What about that reading did you cling to? In what ways did it help you?

5 Have you ever felt a warm glow of peace from God? If so, what were the circumstances? If not, what other ways have you felt God's peace?

Wednesday 24 April

1 When have you felt like you had no hope of succeeding at something? How did you respond? What was the outcome of the situation?

2 How do you encourage those around you to try again even when they don't think they can? How do you help others remember to fix their eyes on God when they feel discouraged or weary?

3 Do you find it hard to do something when you expect to fail? Why or why not? Who or what in your life encourages you to push forward anyway?

4 What does your motivation to keep going look like when you focus on the obstacles in front of you? What does it look like when you are focused on God and God's promises? How does your motivation change based on your focus?

5 What does it mean to you to be surrounded by a great cloud of witnesses? How are you encouraged by them and the people around you to keep running the race marked for you? In what ways do you encourage those around you to do the same?

Journal page

Journal page

Become a Friend of BRF Ministries
and give regularly to support our ministry

We help people of all ages to grow in faith

We encourage and support individual Christians and churches as they
serve and resource the changing spiritual needs of communities today.

Through **Anna Chaplaincy**
we're enabling churches to provide
spiritual care to older people

Through **Living Faith**
we're nurturing faith and resourcing
lifelong discipleship

Through **Messy Church**
we're helping churches to reach out
to families

Through **Parenting for Faith**
we're supporting parents as they raise
their children in the Christian faith

Our ministry is only possible because of the generous support of
individuals, churches, trusts and gifts in wills.

As we look to the future and make plans, **regular donations make a huge
difference** in ensuring we can both start and finish projects well.

By becoming a Friend and giving regularly to our ministry, you are
partnering with us in the gospel and helping change lives.

How your gift makes a difference

£2
a month

Helps us to give away **Living Faith** resources via food banks and chaplaincy services

£10
a month

Helps us to support parents and churches running the **Parenting for Faith** course

£5
a month

Helps us to support **Messy Church** volunteers and grow the wider network

£20
a month

Helps us to develop the reach of **Anna Chaplaincy** and improve spiritual care for older people

How to become a Friend of BRF Ministries

Online – set up a Direct Debit donation at **brf.org.uk/donate** or find out how to set up a Standing Order at **brf.org.uk/friends**

By post – complete and return the form opposite to 'Freepost BRF' (*no other address or stamp is needed*)

If you have any questions, or if you want to change your regular donation or stop giving in the future, do get in touch.

Contact the fundraising team
Email: **giving@brf.org.uk**
Tel: +44 (0)1235 462305
Post: Fundraising team, BRF Ministries,
         15 The Chambers, Vineyard,
         Abingdon OX14 3FE

Registered with

FUNDRAISING
REGULATOR

SHARING OUR VISION – MAKING A GIFT

**I would like to make a donation to support BRF Ministries.
Please use my gift for:**

☐ Where the need is greatest ☐ Anna Chaplaincy ☐ Living Faith

☐ Messy Church ☐ Parenting for Faith

Title	First name/initials	Surname

Address		
		Postcode

Email	

Telephone	

Signature	Date

Our ministry is only possible because of the generous support of individuals,
churches, trusts and gifts in wills.

**Please treat as Gift Aid donations all qualifying
gifts of money made** (*tick all that apply*)

giftaid it

☐ today, ☐ in the past four years, ☐ and in the future.

I am a UK taxpayer and understand that if I pay less Income Tax and/or
Capital Gains Tax in the current tax year than the amount of Gift Aid claimed
on all my donations, it is my responsibility to pay any difference.

☐ My donation does not qualify for Gift Aid.

Please notify us if you want to cancel this Gift Aid declaration, change your name or home
address, or no longer pay sufficient tax on your income and/or capital gains.

You can also give online at **brf.org.uk/donate**, which reduces our administra-
tion costs, making your donation go further.

Please complete other side of this form ➲

Please accept my gift of:

☐ £2 ☐ £5 ☐ £10 ☐ £20 Other £ [   ]

by (*delete as appropriate*):

☐ Cheque/Charity Voucher payable to 'BRF'

☐ MasterCard/Visa/Debit card/Charity card

Name on card

Card no. [ ][ ][ ][ ] [ ][ ][ ][ ] [ ][ ][ ][ ] [ ][ ][ ][ ]

Expires end [M][M] [Y][Y] Security code [ ][ ][ ] Last 3 digits on the reverse of the card

Signature   Date

☐ I would like to leave a gift to BRF Ministries in my will.
Please send me further information.

☐ I would like to find out about giving a regular gift to BRF Ministries.

For help or advice regarding making a gift, please contact
our fundraising team +44 (0)1865 462305

Your privacy

We will use your personal data to process this transaction.
From time to time we may send you information about the
work of BRF Ministries that we think may be of interest to
you. Our privacy policy is available at **brf.org.uk/privacy**.
Please contact us if you wish to discuss your mailing
preferences.

Registered with

FR

FUNDRAISING
REGULATOR

☛ Please complete other side of this form

Please return this form to 'Freepost BRF'
No other address information or stamp is needed

BRF

Bible Reading Fellowship is a charity (233280) and company limited by guarantee (301324),
registered in England and Wales

UR0124

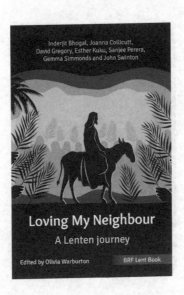

Inderjit Bhogal, Joanna Collicutt,
David Gregory, Esther Kuku, Sanjee Perera,
Gemma Simmonds and John Swinton

Loving My Neighbour

A Lenten journey

Edited by Olivia Warburton

BRF Lent Book

It's never been more important to understand how much God loves us and how much he wants us to love each other. *Loving My Neighbour* takes us on a journey through the challenging terrain of how we can truly love one another, individually and in our communities. Daily Bible readings and reflections from Ash Wednesday to Easter Day explore how we can love in truth, love the vulnerable and the suffering, embrace difference, care for our world, and love ourselves as God loves us.

Loving My Neighbour
A Lenten journey
Inderjit Bhogal, Joanna Collicutt, David Gregory, Esther Kuku,
Sanjee Perera, Gemma Simmonds and John Swinton
978 1 80039 215 1 £9.99
brfonline.org.uk

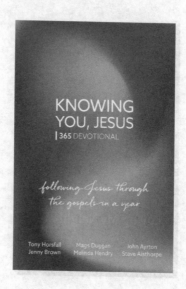

Inspired by the famous prayer of Richard of Chichester 'to see thee more clearly, love thee more dearly and follow thee more nearly... day by day', this 365-day devotional encourages faith formation and intentional discipleship, presenting a detailed, chronological exploration of the life of Jesus of Nazareth, drawing from all four gospels.

Knowing You, Jesus: 365 Devotional
Following Jesus through the gospels in a year
Tony Horsfall, Mags Duggan, John Ayrton, Jenny Brown, Melinda Hendry and Steve Aisthorpe
978 1 80039 185 7 £19.99
brfonline.org.uk

How to encourage Bible reading in your church

BRF Ministries has been helping individuals connect with the Bible for over 100 years. We want to support churches as they seek to encourage church members into regular Bible reading.

Order a Bible reading resources pack

This pack is designed to give your church the tools to publicise our Bible reading notes. It includes:

- Sample Bible reading notes for your congregation to try.
- Publicity resources, including a poster.
- A church magazine feature about Bible reading notes.

The pack is free, but we welcome a £5 donation to cover the cost of postage. If you require a pack to be sent outside the UK or require a specific number of sample Bible reading notes, please contact us for postage costs. For more information about what the current pack contains, go to **brfonline.org.uk/pages/bible-reading-resources-pack**.

How to order and find out more

- Email **enquiries@brf.org.uk**
- Phone us on +44 (0)1865 319700 Mon–Fri 9.30–17.00.
- Write to us at BRF Ministries, 15 The Chambers, Vineyard, Abingdon OX14 3FE.

Keep informed about our latest initiatives

We are continuing to develop resources to help churches encourage people into regular Bible reading, wherever they are on their journey. Join our email list at **brfonline.org.uk/signup** to stay informed about the latest initiatives that your church could benefit from.

Subscriptions

The Upper Room is published in January, May and September.

Individual subscriptions
The subscription rate for orders for 4 or fewer copies includes postage and packing:

The Upper Room annual individual subscription   £19.50

Group subscriptions
Orders for 5 copies or more, sent to ONE address, are post free:
The Upper Room annual group subscription   £14.97

Please do not send payment with order for a group subscription. We will send an invoice with your first order.

Please note that the annual billing period for group subscriptions runs from 1 May to 30 April.

Copies of the notes may also be obtained from Christian bookshops.

Single copies of *The Upper Room* cost £4.99.

Prices valid until 30 April 2025.

Giant print version
The Upper Room is available in giant print for the visually impaired, from:

Torch Trust for the Blind
Torch House
Torch Way
Northampton Road
Market Harborough
LE16 9HL

Tel: +44 (0)1858 438260
torchtrust.org

THE UPPER ROOM: INDIVIDUAL/GIFT SUBSCRIPTION FORM

All our Bible reading notes can be ordered online by visiting brfonline.org.uk/subscriptions

☐ I would like to take out a subscription myself (complete your name and address details once)

☐ I would like to give a gift subscription (please provide both names and addresses)

Title .... First name/initials .... Surname ....

Address ....

.... Postcode ....

Telephone .... Email ....

Gift subscription name ....

Gift subscription address ....

.... Postcode ....

Gift message (20 words max. or include your own gift card):

....

....

Please send *The Upper Room* beginning with the May 2024 / September 2024 / January 2025 issue (*delete as appropriate*):

Annual individual subscription ☐ £19.50

Optional donation* to support the work of BRF Ministries £ ....

Total enclosed £ .... (cheques should be made payable to 'BRF')

*Please complete and return the Gift Aid declaration on page 159 to make your donation even more valuable to us.

Method of payment

Please charge my MasterCard / Visa with £ ....

Card no. ☐☐☐☐ ☐☐☐☐ ☐☐☐☐ ☐☐☐☐

Expires end ☐☐ ☐☐   Security code ☐☐☐   Last 3 digits on the reverse of the card

> **All our Bible reading notes can be ordered online by visiting brfonline.org.uk/subscriptions**

❏ Please send me .... copies of *The Upper Room* May 2024 / September 2024 / January 2025 issue (*delete as appropriate*)

Title .... First name/initials .... Surname ....

Address ....

.... Postcode ....

Telephone .... Email ....

Please do not send payment with this order. We will send an invoice with your first order.

Christian bookshops: All good Christian bookshops stock our resources. For your nearest stockist, please contact us.

Telephone: The BRF office is open Mon–Fri 9.30–17.00. To place your order, telephone +44 (0)1865 319700.

Online: brfonline.org.uk/group-subscriptions

❏ Please send me a Bible reading resources pack to encourage Bible reading in my church

Please return this form with the appropriate payment to:
BRF Ministries, 15 The Chambers, Vineyard, Abingdon OX14 3FE

For terms and cancellation information, please visit **brfonline.org.uk/terms**.

Bible Reading Fellowship is a charity (233280) and company limited by guarantee (301324), registered in England and Wales

UR0124

o order

line: brfonline.org.uk
lephone: +44 (0)1865 319700 Mon–Fri 9.30–17.00

Delivery times within the UK are normally 15 working days. Prices are correct at the time of going to press but may change without prior notice.

itle	Price	Qty	Total
oving My Neighbour (BRF Lent book)	£9.99		
nowing You, Jesus: 365 Devotional	£19.99		

POSTAGE AND PACKING CHARGES			
der value	UK	Europe	Rest of world
nder £7.00	£2.00		
.00–£29.99	£3.00	Available on request	Available on request
0.00 and over	FREE		

Total value of books	
Postage and packing	
Donation*	
Total for this order	

* Please complete the Gift Aid declaration below

ease complete in BLOCK CAPITALS

Title .... First name/initials .... Surname.................................

Address ....

.... Postcode ....

Acc. No. .... Telephone ....

Email ....

Gift Aid Declaration

giftaid it

Please treat as Gift Aid donations all qualifying gifts of money made (*tick all that apply*)
❏ today, ❏ in the past four years, ❏ and in the future **or** ❏ My donation does not qualify for Gift Aid.

am a UK taxpayer and understand that if I pay less Income Tax and/or Capital Gains Tax in the urrent tax year than the amount of Gift Aid claimed on all my donations, it is my responsibility o pay any difference.

Please notify BRF Ministries if you want to cancel this declaration, change your name or home address, or no longer pay sufficient tax on your income and/or capital gains.

Method of payment

❏ Cheque (made payable to BRF) ❏ MasterCard / Visa

Card no. ☐☐☐☐ ☐☐☐☐ ☐☐☐☐ ☐☐☐☐ ☐☐☐☐

Expires end ☐☐ ☐☐ MM YY Security code ☐☐☐ Last 3 digits on the reverse of the card

ease return this form to:

RF Ministries, 15 The Chambers, Vineyard, Abingdon OX14 3FE | **enquiries@brf.org.uk**
r terms and cancellation information, please visit **brfonline.org.uk/terms**.

Bible Reading Fellowship (BRF) is a charity (233280) and company limited by guarantee (301324), registered in England and Wales

Ministries

Inspiring people of all ages to grow in Christian faith

BRF Ministries is the home of Anna Chaplaincy, Living Faith, Messy Church and Parenting for Faith

As a charity, our work would not be possible without fundraising and gifts in wills.

To find out more and to donate, visit brf.org.uk/give or call +44 (0)1235 462305

Registered with FUNDRAISING REGULATOR